Illuminate preaching

The Holy Spirit's vital role in unveiling His Word, the Bible

Jeffrey Crotts

DayOne

© Day One Publications 2010
First printed 2010

ISBN 978–1–84625–166–5

British Library Cataloguing in Publication Data available

Published by Day One Publications
Ryelands Road, Leominster, HR6 8NZ
☎ 01568 613 740 FAX 01568 611 473
email—sales@dayone.co.uk
web site—www.dayone.co.uk
North American—e-mail—sales@dayonebookstore.com
North American—web site—www.dayonebookstore.com

Cover design by Wayne McMaster
Printed by Gutenberg Press, Malta

To my wife Judith, "my beloved and my friend," who both inspired and freed

me hour upon hour to complete this writing endeavor. I could not have done

this without you and in our case you know this is literally true. You have been a

constant support to me, and for this I am exceedingly happy and grateful.

Commendations

I'm thankful for Jeff Crotts' balanced and sharply focused emphasis on the Holy Spirit's illuminating ministry. Two popular misconceptions are afoot in the church today. One is the notion that the Holy Spirit is constantly giving fresh, extrabiblical revelation in the form of personal prophecies. The other is the idea that the Holy Spirit is totally silent. In reality, the Spirit of God is constantly active, always teaching the true church of Christ. He speaks to his people through the Scriptures, enlightening their hearts and minds to understand the truth revealed in the Bible—empowering us to believe and obey it. Illuminated Preaching highlights this role of the Holy Spirit in both the preacher's preparation and the congregation's reception of the Word. Here is a sound, biblical antidote to the shallow superficiality and silly pragmatism that have commandeered so many pulpits today.

John MacArthur, pastor-teacher of Grace Community Church, Sun Valley, California, USA

A commendable balance characterizes the author's efforts and product. By biblically navigating the channel between the reefs of merely academic labors and the shoals of existential subjectivism, he allows the scriptural data to pilot his ship named Illumination to a safe harbor.

Crotts' paradigmatic passage, 2 Corinthians 4:1–6, sets his compass as the ship passes applicationally from condemnation to communication to conversion and finally to convictions. His appendix alone is worth the fare of the book in that it takes his whole reservoir of scriptural data and classifies each passage using a range that spreads all the way from inferential to direct references to illumination.

May this book rescue many contemporary preachers from theologically aberrant methods by the Spirit's illumination of God's words from his Word. May they come to understand where the power of true change comes from and be liberated from ultimately ineffectual tactics.

George J. Zemek, Academic Dean, The Expositors Seminary, USA

Most conservative preachers are familiar to some degree with the doctrine of illumination and realize that in some way it is the ministry of the Holy Spirit. In this book, however, Crotts has made an extensive study of the doctrine, particularly as it relates to the preacher's primary responsibility—to preach the Word. Dividing the doctrine into four categories—condemnation, conversion, communication, and conviction—Crotts takes his reader along with him as he retraces his journey to his present understanding of the doctrine. He shows the importance of the doctrine as it relates to the entire process of preaching—on the part of the preacher in studying the text and communicating the text, and on the part of the hearer in listening to the text which the Holy Spirit uses either in condemnation or conversion. In plain language, Crotts shows how the same sun that melts the butter also hardens the bricks. When the Word of God goes forth the Holy Spirit always sees to it that it accomplishes the purpose which God intended. This book is refreshing because it reminds the preacher that his success is measured not by the size of the crowd, the size of the offering, or the number of people that come forward, but by the ministry of the Holy Spirit in illuminating the preacher, the sermon process, and the hearers.

Paul R. Fink, Th.D., Professor of Biblical Studies and Pastoral Ministry, Liberty University, Lynchburg, Virginia, USA

How often have we as preachers longed for the Holy Spirit's greater power in and through our preaching? (I for one know I have and do!) Additionally, what exactly is this so-called work of the Spirit in bringing the conviction of sin upon human hearts? Even further, how should we rightly conceive of mankind's condemnation without such illumination by the Spirit? Further still, is genuine spiritual conversion even possible without the Holy Spirit's initiative? These critically important questions—and more—are capably answered in Jeff Crotts' book, Illuminated Preaching: The Holy Spirit's Vital Role in Unveiling His Word, the Bible. Using 2 Corinthians 4:1–6 as a key starting point, Pastor Crotts takes us through the entire biblical revelation, showing both explicitly and implicitly how God's Word is to be rightly understood regarding this crucial doctrine of the Spirit's ministry of illumination. If you want to learn how best to rely upon the Holy Spirit's power, including how to trust the Bible to do its work through your own preaching and witnessing to others, then this book is for you! If you sincerely desire to see condemned men and women become convicted of their sin, delivered from eternal doom by the sheer force of the gospel, and then progressively transformed by none other than Jesus Christ, Jeff Crotts is quite prepared from this book to show you how.

Lance Quinn, Pastor-Teacher, The Bible Church of Little Rock, and Professor of Theology, The Expositors Seminary, Little Rock, Arkansas, USA

Commendations

Jeff Crotts reminds us all that the illumination of the Spirit is one of the most liberating and empowering elements of preaching—for pastor and congregant alike. This book, full of biblical insight, historical wisdom, and pastoral warmth, is for all of those clay jars who, week in and week out, proclaim the treasure of the gospel. Here's a preaching manual that goes beneath the surface and speaks straight to the heart.

Stephen J. Nichols, Research Professor of Christianity and Culture, Lancaster Bible College and Graduate School, Lancaster, Pennsylvania, USA

If, as Martin Luther correctly judged, the doctrine of justification is the standing article of the church, I would venture to say that the doctrine of illumination is the standing article of the preacher. Any preacher's ministry stands or falls depending on how real this matter is to him. Therefore, we must thank God for this new and comprehensive treatment of this subject by Jeff Crotts. This truth will keep us from despair when there is hardly any fruit from our preaching, and it will also keep us from pride when God blesses us with abundant fruit. Jeff Crotts shows us that the Spirit's illuminating work is vital because on it hang issues of eternal life and eternal damnation. We cannot afford to be indifferent! I have no doubt that we can only become better preachers by reading this book. We will enter our pulpits as new men, knowing our utter dependence upon the Spirit of the living God and his illuminating work.

Conrad Mbewe, Pastor, Kabwata Baptist Church, Lusaka, Zambia

Spiritual illumination is an absolute necessity for all who preach the Word. Apart from divine enlightenment, the Bible is a closed book, and its preachers are mere blind leaders of the blind. Sadly, countless ministers read, study, and proclaim God's Word without understanding it. Their eyes remain closed to many of its most basic truths. If the Scripture is to be accurately perceived with pinpoint precision, God must illuminate their minds. Divine truth can only be discerned by divine light. The psalmist says, "Open my eyes, that I may behold wondrous things out of your law" (Ps. 119:18). These words must be the constant prayer of every man who steps into the pulpit. Jeffrey Crotts has done the church a wonderful service in preparing this book, Illuminated Preaching, which provides a constructive study on this vitally important subject. I am convinced you will find this book to be a valuable tool in gaining insight into the illuminating work of the Holy Spirit in preaching.

Dr. Steven J. Lawson, Senior Pastor, Christ Fellowship Baptist Church, Mobile, Alabama, USA

Contents

Foreword

I have often wondered how it is that the Holy Spirit can take any sermon of mine and make something—anything—even remotely powerful out of it! Have you ever had that same kind of thought? You desire to see people respond to your preaching. You seek to have men and women convicted and changed through the saving gospel. You work diligently to bring sinners to repentance and believers to greater levels of holiness. But how does all this actually come to pass? What are the keys to understanding how the Holy Spirit brings any of this to fruition? The Bible's own answer is this: If indeed there is to be any lasting spiritual fruit in our preparing and preaching of biblical sermons, it will only come as a direct result of the Spirit's illumination of the human heart. If any spiritually blind eyes are to be opened, if any spiritually deaf ears are to be unstopped, if spiritually dead people are ever to be regenerated and granted spiritual life in Christ, it will occur solely because the Holy Spirit has sovereignly used his own inspired Word to grant them that life. When you and I as ministers of the gospel look and long to have effective ministries of communication, it will only come from the sovereign prerogative of the Holy Spirit himself to give us any success to our labors in the Word. That's why I am excited about this book, *Illuminated Preaching: The Holy Spirit's Vital Role in Unveiling His Word, the Bible*, for in it, Jeff Crotts, a close pastoral colleague of mine for well over a decade, has succinctly but capably captured the essence of how to understand the Holy Spirit's presence and role in using Holy Scripture to give sight to the blind, hearing to the deaf, and genuine spiritual life to the walking dead.

All preachers have no doubt often descended from the pulpit after preaching and longed for the Holy Spirit's greater power in and through their preaching. We believe in the power of the Spirit and we are committed to the sufficiency of God's Word, but what is the real, spiritual dynamic going on as we preach? What will be its effect? Additionally, what exactly is this so-called work of the Spirit in bringing the conviction of sin upon human hearts? Even further, how should we rightly conceive of mankind's condemnation without such illumination by the Spirit? Further still, is genuine spiritual conversion even possible without the Holy Spirit's initiative? These critically important questions—and more—are capably answered in the book you now hold in your hands. Using 2 Corinthians

4:1–6 as a key starting point, Pastor Crotts takes us through the entire biblical revelation, showing both explicitly and implicitly how God's Word is to be rightly understood regarding this crucial doctrine of the Spirit's ministry of illumination. By providing a helpful, synthesized overview of the biblical theology of illumination, and then giving us a pertinent historical context for how others have understood the doctrine of illumination, Dr. Crotts bases his argument for the precise biblical and theological understanding of the doctrine by using four separate but interrelated terms which give us a handle upon which to grasp these important truths regarding Spirit-engendered illumination: *condemnation, communication, conversion,* and *convictions.* He has made his case, I think, and, to my mind, made it quite well.

If you have ever struggled with precisely how your own preaching of the Bible might have an effect on your hearers—let alone yourself—you are in store for an informed and affirming read. If you want to learn how best to rely upon the Holy Spirit's power in your preaching, including how to trust the Bible to do its work through you, then this book is truly for you! If you sincerely desire to see condemned men and women become convicted of their sin, delivered from eternal doom by the sheer force of the gospel, and then progressively transformed by none other than Jesus Christ, Jeff Crotts is quite prepared from this book to show you how.

Lance Quinn
Pastor-Teacher, The Bible Church of Little Rock
and Professor of Theology, The Expositors Seminary, Little Rock, Arkansas, USA

When I was seven my family attended a small Baptist church, and my first memory of understanding illumination comes from the close of one particular service there. The congregation was singing "Turn Your Eyes upon Jesus" (Helen H. Lemmel) and these words from the chorus touched my tender young heart: "Turn your eyes upon Jesus/Look full in his wonderful face/And the things of earth will grow strangely dim/In the light of his glory and grace." I was moved, but I also understood that this "seeing" of Jesus meant something other than physically seeing him in front of me—it was a spiritual seeing. I understood this to be believing and seeing Jesus by faith, the essence of spiritual illumination.

Nearly a decade later, and as a newly converted teenager, I remember thinking through this concept again from a different vantage point. My family was now attending a different Baptist church, and I was challenged, in a way very similar to when I was seven, to think at the close of a service. We were ending our annual evangelistic concert and I remember being stunned by something my worship pastor said. As was his custom, he concluded the event by making an appeal to those in attendance to believe in Jesus as their personal Savior. On this particular evening, instead of quoting a classic gospel passage like John 3:16 or Acts 16:31, he chose to paraphrase the French philosopher Blaise Pascal. Pascal said, "Belief is a wise wager ... faith cannot be proved, [so] what harm will come to you if you gamble on its truth and it proves false? If you gain, you gain all; if you lose, you lose nothing. Wager, then, without hesitation, that He exists."[1]

I was very young in the Lord, and hearing this from one of my pastors made me feel weak and kind of sick inside. What kind of Christianity was this man promoting? It appeared to me that he was presenting coming to Christ as some kind of gamble, and that he had no settled assurance. This approach seemed ridiculous to me, probably due to the fact that I was such a new believer, had just been snatched out of a rebellious lifestyle, and was so keenly aware of the transformation that had taken place in my life. I was certain that I stood on a significantly more solid foundation than a mere philosophical gamble. I was not yet schooled in the doctrine of the Spirit, but I remember sitting in that service with a fundamental clarity over this issue and a deep assurance that God had made me his own and I was going to heaven. I knew that my conversion had been a work of God, not some kind of wager.

Twenty years later I found myself face to face once again with the reality of illumination. As a pastor to a group of young adults, I was sitting in my office with a young couple having an informal visit to get to know one another better. I wanted to hear from them how their dating relationship was going. I did not have an easy, natural way to break into conversation, so since I really did not know how these two were doing spiritually—or, to be honest, whether or not they were genuine believers—I decided to simply ask them to share their personal testimonies. What they began to share both surprised and humbled me, as they each, in their own words, connected their conversions to our young adults' Bible study of the previous summer, when I had taught a topical series on the theme of "godliness."

I was stunned. All I could think of while they were telling me of their conversions was how weak I thought my presentations of the Word had been that summer. Of course I understood that God saves people by his grace, but my sermons had just been so bland! My content was biblical, and I was convinced of the truth of what I was saying, but I knew that at the time I had felt that my teaching had not come off particularly well. As they spoke of their new growing relationships in the Lord, I listened gratefully, with a lump in my throat, and concluded one thing: The power that saved them was obviously not from me. The apostle Paul summarized my experience perfectly when he wrote to the Corinthian believers, saying, "… my speech and my message were not in plausible words of wisdom, but in demonstration of the Spirit and of power, that your faith might not rest in the wisdom of men but in the power of God" (1 Cor. 2:4–5). Paul knew that the power of God never came through slick communication skills, but rather by the Spirit of God. God is the one who saves, and the Spirit of God did his work through the Word of God.

A growing understanding of the significance of illumination has compelled me to search the Scriptures to better clarify and understand this biblical doctrine, and this study has been nothing less than amazing. Grasping this truth as it is laid out in the Bible has crystallized for me what occurred during my salvation, as well as what my role is now as a pastor who communicates God's truth. In this aspect, my study has been quite liberating.

Understanding the role of the Holy Spirit in preaching has in some ways taken pressure off, and in other ways put more on. In terms of the act of preaching, I sense less pressure as I have come to recognize that it is up to the Holy Spirit to open people's spiritual eyes to the truths presented in a sermon. At the same time, this doctrine increased pressure for me as I began to understand how crucial it is to accurately interpret and present the Scriptures with the recognition that the instrument the Spirit uses to illumine people is his Word. Instead of placing the emphasis on great communication, my goal is to remove any obstacles that muddy the clarity of the truth I present so as to promote the Spirit's role of illumination.

Accountability has increased for me, not just as a preacher, but also as a Christian. I understand my need to have personal integrity to first seek God before seeking to be illumined in study. As a communicator it is no longer sufficient for me to focus simply on right interpretation and preparation of a passage. I should never settle for mere accuracy—I must have the Holy Spirit's illumination. I need the Spirit first to illumine to my own heart the text I am planning to preach, so that my own life may be transformed by my preaching preparation. This is a call for authenticity and personal integrity in the pastor's study. The words of my homiletics mentor from college still ring in my ears: "It is not how many times you go through the Word, but how many times the Word goes through you." My focus in sermonic preparation has become more God-centered.

I do not believe that this emphasis now gives me the excuse to be passive and say, "Well, since it is not up to my speaking ability, I will just coast through my sermon." Nor do I think I should remove all personality from my delivery, that a mark of being really deep or spiritual is to be boring in the pulpit. This emphasis, this call for illumination, actually raises the bar and sets a higher standard for the preparation process and delivery of the sermon. The challenge to be first illumined by the Spirit of God is the challenge to work more diligently, not only in the aspects of critical study and communication, but also in spending time in spiritual meditation on the text. I must engage with the particular passage on a heart level. A true understanding of illumination does not allow for sermon preparation to be solely academic, a merely perfunctory exercise. Instead, I must come to my study as a matter of personal sanctification, begging God and saying, "Open my eyes, that I may behold wondrous things out of your law" (Ps. 119:18).

Make no mistake—this adds pressure to the preparation. But isn't it worth it? Being illumined by the text before preaching it is truly the essence of being an authentic communicator. More often than not, those listening can sense when I have been affected by the text I am preaching. This not only makes for powerful preaching, it also models the very thing that I desire to see happen in the hearts of those who are hearing.

Notes

1. **Blaise Pascal,** *Pensées*, trans. **W. F. Trotter** (New York: Random House, 1941), p. 81.

An overview of a synthesized biblical theology of illumination from 2 Corinthians 4:1–6

The term "illumination," if looked up in a book about systematic theology, hermeneutics, or preaching, will typically have just a small section devoted to it, maybe only a simple definition of the work of the Spirit in the life of the believer. I was generally dissatisfied by the material available on the subject, and before beginning this study I believed that much of what was written merely scratched the surface, especially in terms of living the Christian life. For me to be sure of this—to be convinced of its breadth and significance and to truly get a handle on what illumination is—I needed to comprehensively search the sixty-six books of the Bible to see what I would find.

So I did. I used a standard Bible software program[1] and traced key words, words with either a direct or indirect bearing upon the Holy Spirit's work of illumining the minds of people, from Genesis to Revelation. Some of the words I surveyed were the following: spirit, spiritual, Holy Spirit, discern, perceive, discretion, witness, eye, ear, hear, taste, reveal, revelation, wisdom, knowledge, enlightening, light, meditate, and testimony. I then categorized them under their particular Bible books. This project turned into what amounts to a biblical theology, or survey and analysis of this doctrine. I then analyzed each verse in its individual context, determining whether it contained a direct or indirect bearing upon this doctrine. This aspect of the project became the meat of this book. (The notes from my study can be found in the Appendix.)

This study did not disappoint. I saw quickly that the doctrine of illumination spanned Scripture, and I was convinced that God had clearly revealed, in a variety of ways and in a variety of Bible books, that he illumines people with his Word. Four categories began to emerge as a way for me to classify these scriptural references regarding illumination. The first, *condemnation*, refers to the person who is without illumination, the one who is rejecting the Word of God. The second, *conversion*, speaks of the transformation that takes place when God transforms a heart by illumination. The third, *communication*, speaks of how prophets, preachers, and evangelists communicate God's Word, which is the means of illumination. The fourth, *conviction*, refers to the process whereby believers are enriched in their own spiritual walks as they gain certainty about biblical truth as the Spirit illumines the Word.

These four categories clarified for me that spiritual illumination is much more than simply knowing God more deeply by gaining new insights from studying the Bible. Spiritual growth is a part of the discussion of illumination, but its beginning point is salvation. Illumined people are genuine Christians; those without illumination are not. This is a serious doctrine. The Bible's teaching about illumination goes well beyond the idea of getting to know the Bible better; it shows that illumination has eternal consequences: spiritual life and death. The Bible draws a clear line—a person has either been illumined by the Holy Spirit or not, and on this basis is either growing in grace or not. I believe that it is because of the serious nature of this doctrine that it is woven throughout the entire biblical record.

Although I found these categories expressed throughout the whole of Scripture, I also discovered that they are crystallized in a single paragraph of the New Testament, 2 Corinthians 4:1–6. No other passage in the entire Bible so succinctly captures these four themes of illumination, so I will briefly survey these verses in order to lay a foundation for this study. This way, the Scriptures serve as both foundation and launching pad as we open up each category.

The apostle Paul, author of 2 Corinthians, begins this particular passage by setting the stage, providing a context for his teaching on illumination. Here, as throughout the letter, Paul expresses his desire that this church clearly understand that his apostolic ministry is one of self-deprecation. He wants his readers to understand that he acknowledges the source of spiritual power for his ministry to be God, not himself.

The context

Therefore, having this ministry by the mercy of God, we do not lose heart. But we have renounced disgraceful, underhanded ways. We refuse to practice cunning or to tamper with God's word, but by the open statement of the truth we would commend ourselves to everyone's conscience in the sight of God. (2 Cor. 4:1–2)

These lead-in verses clearly show that Paul gave all credit for his ministry in the life of this church to God. Essentially, he was labeling his preaching opportunity an undeserved gift. He called it a "ministry by the mercy of God." Paul never forgot who he was before he was rescued and transformed into a follower of Christ. This is one of many references to his pre-conversion state that Paul made throughout his writings. Reading Paul, one can sense that he never forgot how utterly lost and sinful he was before Christ found him and saved him.

With this as his backdrop, Paul tells the Corinthians that he is clear in his conscience—he knows that he has never manipulated his hearers as a gospel preacher. Where does this kind of humility come from? I believe that in Paul's case it came from his awareness not only of his past, but also of this essential work of spiritual illumination that makes preaching effective.

Theme 1: Condemnation without illumination

And even if our gospel is veiled, it is veiled only to those who are perishing. In their case the god of this world has blinded the minds of the unbelievers, to keep them from seeing the light of the gospel of the glory of Christ, who is the image of God.

(2 Cor. 4:3–4)

Paul understood the work of illumination, which gave him clarity about why people spurn the gospel. He did not blame himself or his preaching for their rejection, knowing that, no matter how effective a communicator he was, no spiritual life could or would be produced apart from God's spiritual intervention. Here in verses 3 and 4 Paul puts the blame where it belongs. People reject truth because they are spiritually dead, because they are "perishing." He says that for those who are in this desperate spiritual state the "gospel is veiled." By saying this he does not mean that people cannot physically read or hear gospel content, but that for them this message has been rendered insignificant, without value. Paul explains this in terms of Satan's soul-destroying influence, pointing out that "the god of this world" blinds people's minds. Satan is a schemer and liar (John 8:44; Eph. 6:11) who is committed to facilitating gospel rejection by shrouding the Lord's saving light, keeping spiritually dead people dead. Perishing people are blind, and unable to see and taste the glory and beauty of God that fires the soul through the work of the Spirit. To use a musical metaphor, it is as if, when the glorious gospel song is sung, Satan flips a distortion switch in the ears of the perishing so that the music sounds ugly, twisted, and unattractive.

Theme 2: Communication for illumination

For what we proclaim is not ourselves, but Jesus Christ as Lord, with ourselves as your servants for Jesus' sake. (2 Cor. 4:5)

Here Paul, speaking again in humility, reveals how God has designed for a person's spiritual blinders to be removed, for his or her spiritual fog or cloud of darkness to be lifted. This enlightening was not dependent upon Paul's communication style or ability, but simply upon preaching. Proclamation of truth has been the fundamental way of giving the gospel since the inception of the church (Acts 2:14), yet in search of relevancy believers may find it easy to set aside or even replace this method (see 2 Tim. 4:1–4).

Paul here emphasizes the content preached—"not ourselves" but the simple gospel truth of "Jesus Christ as Lord"—even more than the method. Preaching Jesus is the ancient and historic form of biblical communication, a form rooted first in biblical history and then in church tradition. Preaching has its moorings in the visions and revelations proclaimed by the Old Testament prophets, men tasked as heralds of God and spokesmen to his people and to unbelieving nations. These prophets modeled the method by foreshadowing and pointing to Christ, creating the foundation for the early church (Eph. 2:20).

Since "Jesus as Lord" is the essential message, and this message is by nature authoritative, preaching becomes a very appropriate primary method. Paul makes it clear that it is this gospel message—not just any message—that transforms dead souls. This is why the apostle Peter calls the gospel the "imperishable" seed, the change-agent which germinates in the soul, causing life (1 Peter 1:23). When this transformation takes place Jesus reigns as Lord in the hearts of new believers. They are delivered from death's darkness and enlightened in their souls to see the face of Christ.

Theme 3: Conversion by illumination

For God, who said, "Let light shine out of darkness," has shone in our hearts …

(2 Cor. 4:6)

Paul knew that it is no less a miracle for God to create spiritual light in a person who is "perishing" and "blinded" than for God to create the heavens and the earth from nothing. Paul clearly demonstrated that illumination is a creative event. When Paul wrote that God said, "Let light shine out of darkness," he referred all the way back to the beginning of time as documented in Genesis 1:1–3, where Moses wrote, "In the beginning, God created the heavens and the earth. The earth was without form and void, and darkness was over the face of the deep. And the Spirit of God was hovering over the face of the waters. And God said, 'Let there be light.'" This was not an allusion or vague reference to the creation event, but a direct comparison of spiritual conversion to physical creation.

Conversion is what takes place when people in a state of perishing come to know the glorious light of the gospel; it is the point at which God creates life in the otherwise spiritually dead and doomed soul. Conversion should be viewed as the beginning of illumination in a person's life. All things pertaining to this gift of illumination flow out of the creative event of conversion. Paul describes this spiritual transformation as the beginning, the source of all subsequent blessings, which we will refer to as the spiritual convictions gained throughout the Christian's experience.

Theme 4: Convictions gained by illumination

… to give the light of the knowledge of the glory of God in the face of Jesus Christ.

(2 Cor. 4:6)

Paul depicts conversion as a saving event whereby a spiritually blind person experiences initial illumination—but he does not stop there. He goes on to speak of the fruit of conversion, the illumined convictions that he calls "knowledge." When Paul says that God gives "the light of the knowledge," he is not talking about bookish academic knowledge; rather, he is speaking of what a person in the deepest part of his or her being now affirms as unequivocally true. This person now possesses deep heartfelt certainty regarding biblical truth.

The "knowledge" or conviction of which Paul speaks is "of the glory of God," specifically "in the face of Jesus Christ." Obviously Paul is not saying that newly illumined people physically see an image of the shining glorious Jesus Christ in their minds. Notice again how Paul uses the term "knowledge" to describe what happens in a person's soul. This person supernaturally gains something. He or she gains spiritual "knowledge"; he or she "knows the truth" (see John 8:32). In the case of 2 Corinthians 4:6, the believer is illumined to know, by conviction, that the glory of God is shining forth from the Son of God. Illumined believers see and taste glory because the Spirit has recalibrated their minds and affections to form a conviction that they have found the authentic Christ. They would stake their lives on it.

While a person receives illumined "knowledge" at conversion, the Bible also teaches that all believers should "grow in the grace and *knowledge* of our Lord and Savior Jesus Christ" (2 Peter 3:18) until they reach heaven. We will look at this more closely later in the context of Chapter 6. It is these illumined convictions that measure a person's relationship to Christ and spiritual maturity (2 Cor. 3:18; Col. 1:9–10).

I want to challenge the common perception that illumination is simply a way by which God enhances personal Bible study. These four categories reveal the weight and breadth of this doctrine. My hope is that these biblical truths will challenge and perhaps redefine the way the Christian life is understood, as well as the mission of the communicator of truth. For the preacher, meditation on biblical illumination may serve to open a window into the spiritual realm so that what is truly at stake in the preparation and preaching of God's Word becomes apparent. Let us see, with eyes spiritually aware, that those who are blind to the Spirit's illumination are *condemned*, that the gospel *communication* is the only hope a person has for being illumined, that when a person is initially illumined his or her soul is actually being *converted*, and, once that person is converted, *convictions* are gained throughout the Christian life by means of illumination.

Note

1 *BibleWorks 6: Software for Biblical Exegesis and Research*, CD-ROM (Norfolk, VA: BibleWorks, LLC, 2005).

The historical context for a biblical theology of illumination

Throughout church history men of God have recognized the significance of this doctrine that is so widely found throughout the Word. Understanding the reality and importance of illumination drove the church in the early 16th century to value the expository preaching of men such as Martin Luther and John Calvin. Puritan writers like John Owen and others were profoundly influenced by the doctrine of illumination, as evidenced by the way it flows in and through their writings and reflections.[1] Jonathan Edwards, the great American preacher and theologian from the 18th century, was another man of God whose writings and thoughts were permeated with this doctrine. It has been said that for one to truly understand Edwards' apologetics, sermons, and teachings, one must first grasp his understanding of the doctrine of illumination.[2]

The man who stands out as a forerunner in crystallizing the teaching of illumination is John Calvin. Reading his testimony, it is readily apparent that this doctrine meant a great deal to him. When Calvin was a young man in the early 1500s, a significant transition was taking place across Europe. Throughout the Middle Ages God's Word had been held at a distance from the common man by the established church, resulting in massive spiritual darkness in the world. Most people did not have access to God's Word because it was not translated into the common tongue. The Bible was unreadable and impossible to understand; however, with the Protestant Reformation, all this changed. Access to the Bible was gained. In fact, one of the heart-cries of the Protestant Reformation was the slogan *post tenebras lux*: "After darkness, light." This light was the spiritual light of illumination believers receive from God's Word. At this point in history, through the Word being preached and read, spiritual awakening came with blinding brilliance and spread the gospel across the globe.

Calvin understood well the need for people to be illumined, so from the very start of his ministry in Geneva he was committed to expository preaching, as was reflected in his work ethic. He was a busy pastor. His time was filled with counseling, visiting sick members, writing letters, officiating at public ceremonies such as weddings, baptisms, and the Lord's Table, as well as with the private duty of praying for his flock. He was, however, first and foremost a preacher. He devoted much of his time to studying his Bible, preparing to preach two sermons every Sunday plus one sermon every day of the week on alternating weeks. Every two weeks Calvin was preaching, on average, nine to ten times. He also taught as a theological professor and preached to and mentored local Genevan pastors on Fridays. So in a typical year, Calvin preached about 286 sermons.3 It has been said that Calvin's elders insisted upon this rigorous preaching program so that the light from his preaching would effect change in the surrounding Genevan culture.4 While this arduous preaching schedule must have been physically demanding, his elders gave good counsel. The light from his pulpit ministry is still shining around the world today.

For Calvin, this was not an unwelcome requirement because he understood the doctrine of illumination well. Throughout his *Institutes* and sermons runs the teaching of what he called "the internal testimony of the Holy Spirit," which is the *certainty* of the Scripture confirmed by the Spirit in the heart of the believer. Calvin also called this "the internal witness of the Spirit" or the "enlightenment" that comes through "the medium of verbal testimony [where a believer's] blind eyes of the spirit are opened, and divine realities come to be recognized and embraced for what they are."5 He was so convinced of the reality of the "inward persuasion of the Holy Spirit"6 that he compared it to his physical experience, saying illumination was "… as immediate and unanalysable as the perceiving of a color, or a taste, by physical sense … [that] when it happened [a person knew] … it had happened."7 Calvin clearly stated that the testimonium, or this witness of the Spirit, was not some kind of additional revelation beyond the Scripture. He says, "Therefore the Spirit, promised to us, has not the task of inventing new and unheard-of revelations, or of forging a new kind of doctrine, to lead us away from the received doctrine of the gospel, but of sealing our minds [the testimonium] with that very doctrine which is commended by the gospel."[8]

The Spirit's work "… awakens us, as from the dead, to see and taste the divine reality of God in Scripture, which authenticates it as God's own word."[9] Again, for Calvin, the Word of God is saving, but is made certain by the "inward persuasion of the Holy Spirit."[10] So a person illumined will automatically have the perspective that Scripture "wins reverence for itself by its own majesty … illumined by its power, we believe …; but above human judgment we affirm with utter certainty (just as if we were gazing upon the majesty of God himself) that it has flowed to us from the very mouth of God …"[11] Calvin declared this as "more excellent than reason," when, by the sealing work of the Spirit, the Bible obtains full "acceptance" in a person's heart.[12]

Reading Calvin's testimony of his conversion makes it easy to understand why this doctrine meant so much to him. For Calvin, this teaching framed his personal experience of becoming a Christian. While the exact date of his conversion is not known, some time after 1533 Calvin described his own original illumination that took place while he was still a practicing Catholic. What is noteworthy is how he measured the authenticity of his conversion in terms of the spiritual light that caused his mind and affections to be moved by the Word. Calvin describes this thus:

… A very different form of doctrine started up, not one which led us away from the Christian profession, but one which brought it back to its fountain … to its original purity. Offended by the novelty, I lent an unwilling ear, and at first, I confess, strenuously and passionately resisted … to confess that I had all my life long been in ignorance and error … I at length perceived, as if *light* had broken in upon me, in what a sty of error I had wallowed, and how much pollution and impurity I had thereby contracted. Being exceedingly alarmed at the misery into which I had fallen … as in duty bound, [I] made it my first business to betake myself to thy way [O God], condemning my past life, not without groans and tears. God, by a sudden conversion subdued and brought my mind to a teachable frame … Having thus received some taste and knowledge of true godliness, I was immediately inflamed with [an] intense desire to make progress.[13]

He was given spiritual eyesight and he suddenly embraced the truth for what it was—the revelation of God. He had discovered the certainty of Scripture by what he called "the secret testimony of the Spirit" or "the inward persuasion of the Holy Spirit." It is no overstatement to say that his understanding of this doctrine was what drove his ministry in the Word. Why else would John Calvin have given his life to expository preaching? Calvin knew that God's light only shines in a person's soul through the vehicle of biblical truth, and so he devoted his entire life to exegetical study from the Hebrew and Greek Scriptures.[14] History makes it clear that his preaching ministry influenced his own culture, with the effects felt far beyond—reaching even down to today. Calvin maintained the simple commitment to preach truth to his community in Geneva about three out of every four days—all with the purpose of bringing light!

What Calvin called the "testimonium" should be categorically understood as an "application" of the general doctrine of illumination.[15] For this reason, Calvin is a foundational theologian for the development of this doctrine as a whole.

Let us be clear about what I am *not* saying in this book. I am not suggesting that the Holy Spirit is somehow imprisoned by the Word of God.[16] Rather, I am emphasizing that again and again I find in Scripture that, in terms of illumination, the same Holy Spirit who inspired the Word (2 Tim. 3:16; 2 Peter 1:21) "works with the Word (*cum verbo*) and through the Word (*per verbum*), not without or apart from the Word (*sine verbo*)."[17]

On a personal note, my purpose for writing on illumination is more than the fact that I find it fascinating. I want to show that understanding this doctrine is essential to effectively communicate truth. Though the Bible is replete with examples of this teaching, we will journey through just some of the mountain peaks of illumination from the Scripture, surveying them through the lens of our four main categories—condemnation, communication, conversion, and convictions. I would encourage you to read not just as Bible communicators but as ordinary Christians. Allow the biblical references to prompt your own personal examination. Ask yourself, "Am I in light or darkness?" and "Am I growing closer to Christ as the Spirit opens my eyes to truth?"

Notes

1 **Stephen J. Nichols,** *An Absolute Sort of Certainty: The Holy Spirit and the Apologetics of Jonathan Edwards* (Phillipsburg, NJ: P & R, 2003), p. 47.

2 Ibid. pp. 175–177.

3 **David L. Larsen,** *The Company of Preachers: A History of Biblical Preaching from the Old Testament to the Modern Era* (Grand Rapids, MI: Kregel, 1998), p. 167.

4 **Walter Kaiser,** "The Power of the Word of God," sermon preached at The Bible Church of Little Rock, October 22, 2006, at: http://64.19.50.210/Default.aspx.

5 **J. I. Packer,** "Calvin the Theologian," in **G. E. Duffield,** (ed.), *John Calvin: A Collection of Essays* (London: Sutton Courtenay Press, 1966), p. 166.

6 **John Calvin, John T. McNeill,** (ed.), and **Ford Lewis Battles,** (tr.), *Calvin: Institutes of the Christian Religion,* vols. XX and XXI of **John Baillie, John T. McNeill,** and **Henry P. Van Dusen,** (eds.), *The Library of Christian Classics* (Louisville, KY: Westminster John Knox Press, 1960), p. 80.

7 **Packer,** "Calvin the Theologian," p. 166.

8 **Calvin,** *Institutes,* p. 94.

9 **Packer,** "Calvin the Theologian," p. 166.

10 Ibid. p. 92.

11 Ibid. p. 80.

12 Ibid. p. 79.

13 Quoted in **John Dillenberger,** (ed.), Introduction, *John Calvin: Selections from his Writings* ([n.p.]: Scholars Press for the American Academy of Religion, 1975), p. 26.

14 Ibid. p. 14.

15 **J. I. Packer,** *God Has Spoken* (Grand Rapids, MI: Baker, 1988), p. 132.

16 **Hendrikus Berkhof,** *The Doctrine of the Holy Spirit: The Annie Kinkead Warfield Lectures, 1963–1964* (Richmond, VA: John Knox Press, 1964), p. 38.

17 **R. C. Sproul,** "The Internal Testimony of the Holy Spirit," in **Norman L. Geisler,** (ed.), *Inerrancy* (Grand Rapids, MI: Zondervan, 1980), p. 338 (based on the work of **G. C. Berkouwer,** *Die Heilige Schrift,* 2 vols. (Kampen: Kok, 1966), 1:74).

Condemnation without illumination

I n order to understand what it means to be illumined by the Spirit, it is important to first understand why some are not illumined. Paul speaks of this when he says the "… gospel is veiled … [and] the god of this world has blinded the minds of the unbelievers …" (2 Cor. 4:3–4). Unbelievers have a veil, or shroud of darkness, over their minds that spiritually blinds them to the *truthfulness* of truth. The unbeliever is powerless to see the glory of Christ. As we saw in Chapter 1, Paul specifically attributes this blindness to the god of this world, Satan, also known as "the prince of the power of the air" (Eph. 2:2). He is the one responsible for unbelievers being stupefied by and unable to spiritually apprehend the gospel (2 Cor. 4:4), thereby keeping them from turning to the Lord (2 Cor. 3:16).

If God's sovereignty, his absolute rule (see Ps. 103:19; Rom. 8:28), is understood, then it follows that God is ultimately controlling and allowing for all things to take place. By implication, this means that God is permitting Satan to play this role of blocking the gospel. Why would God allow this? The future is so bleak for unbelievers. All without illumination are blind, presently under condemnation, and even on this side of eternity are already "perishing" (2 Cor. 4:3). This sounds as if it would be at cross-purposes with God's desire for mankind to be saved (2 Peter 3:9), but is it really?

Old Testament passages
Throughout the biblical record God gives clear indication as to why so many are blind to the truth. A reading of the Old Testament shows that God's own chosen nation, Israel, was more often in spiritual darkness than in spiritual light. Israel ignored the prophets who warned them and instead ran after temporal lusts and the worship of false gods.

One of the seasons of straying is documented in 1 Samuel 3:1, where the prophet writes, "And the word of the LORD was rare in those days; there was no frequent vision." As the story goes, the reason why God was withholding blessing was because of corruption in Israel's spiritual leadership, specifically in the priesthood. Those who were expected to be most holy, those supposed to lead people to worship the one true God, were themselves ruled by their lust.

This is the backdrop to the story of Samuel's call. Think of how God called Samuel to serve as both priest and prophet in 1 Samuel 3. Remember how Samuel's mother Hannah had dedicated her son to be raised from infancy to be a priest? He was living near the tabernacle, learning from his mentor, Eli, who, though he held the position of priest, had some serious parenting issues. Eli's sons, Hophni and Phinehas, were so sinful that the Bible labels them as "worthless." They conducted priestly ministry in demanding and self-serving ways (1 Sam. 2:12–17) and "did not know the LORD" (1 Sam. 2:12). Both were involved in immorality, which clearly disqualified them from the priesthood, and in God's eyes they deserved death (1 Sam. 2:25).

According to 1 Samuel 3:1, the patterns of sin in the lives of these men meant that for the nation of Israel "… the word of the LORD was rare in those days; there was no frequent vision." God's people had their lifeline of communication with God severed. Hearing from God was rare. The satellite system was on the blink and the television showed only snow. Though Samuel was stationed near the tabernacle, the place designed to be the center of the worship of the LORD, he too was bereft of God's fellowship because of the poor state of things, since "the word of the LORD had not yet been revealed to him" (1 Sam. 3:7).

Thankfully, the story does not end there. The LORD revealed himself to Samuel, and did so while he was still a young boy. Upon hearing from God, Samuel declared himself to be the LORD's slave. He was now the one who "heard" God's Word (1 Sam. 3:10–11). Later, he grew to be known not only as a priest but also as a prophet when, once again, "… the LORD revealed himself to Samuel at Shiloh by the word of the LORD" (1 Sam. 3:21). These revelations, first coming to Samuel and then ultimately to the nation through his prophetic ministry, changed the spiritual direction of Israel—God was again speaking to them.

From this narrative it is apparent that sin is a barrier to illumination. Though this seems obvious, it is nevertheless sobering and is a principle that can easily be forgotten. In 2 Corinthians 4, Satan is shown to be the blinder. Here in 1 Samuel 3, the root of the spiritual blindness is sin. The influences of Satan and sin form a biblical tension that comes up throughout Scripture (see Eph. 2:1–3; James 4:1–7).

Sin is what makes people hard-hearted toward God and renders them spiritually blind and deaf to his revelation. They are objects of the Lord's condemnation. Remember when the LORD called Isaiah into prophetic ministry? Isaiah was the LORD's spokesman during some of Israel's most unholy days. Isaiah 6:1 recounts that Judah's King Uzziah died and Isaiah went into the temple to seek the LORD on behalf of the nation. At that moment he was swept up into a heavenly vision, in which he saw the exalted LORD. Suddenly being in God's holy presence crushed him with guilt and despair. The passage describes Isaiah as feeling completely "lost," or, more literally, as if he was disintegrating or "ceasing" to exist. Isaiah saw no hope for restoration in his self-pronounced "woe" judgment, which meant he understood himself to be condemned (Isa. 6:5). He confessed, "I am a man of unclean lips, and I dwell in the midst of a people of unclean lips." In his case the LORD granted grace, honoring his contrite response not merely by restoring him, but also by issuing a call for him to preach. Without hesitation, Isaiah accepted (Isa. 6:8).

The picture of a man of God signing up to preach for God is not new or unusual. What is striking here is the goal God set for Isaiah's ministry. His primary ministry objective was not pretty. The LORD assigned this preacher to the task of being a messenger who, for the most part, would always be rejected. His gospel ministry would mostly result in death, not life. In other words, he preached for the purpose of condemnation. When Isaiah first heard God's summary of what his preaching ministry was going to be like, it must have been discouraging:

And he said, "Go, and say to this people:
'Keep on hearing, but do not understand;
keep on seeing, but do not perceive.'
Make the heart of this people dull,

and their ears heavy,
    and blind their eyes;
lest they see with their eyes,
    and hear with their ears,
and understand with their hearts,
    and turn and be healed."   (Isa. 6:9–10)

Anyone hearing this call would be tempted to say, "Wait a minute, I'm not sure what I just agreed to do." Isaiah's preaching was first and foremost a ministry of condemnation—preaching to cause spiritual blindness.

This is not the reason why preachers usually go to seminary. Keep in mind the core issue, though. People are born in sin, and their rejection of God warrants condemnation. It is very clear from Isaiah 5 that Israel and Judah, at this point in biblical history, were rebellious and deserving of these woe judgments. Because of Israel's sin, God's Word fell mostly on deaf ears. They were not illumined to hear it, even though they were the chosen nation. A reading of the Old Testament shows that Israel's spiritual track record was a roller-coaster ride. They wavered between belief and unbelief, between spiritual life and spiritual death. One example of a low point comes from the prophet Hosea, who reproached Israel for their immorality, calling them "a people without understanding" (Hosea 4:14). The prophet Zechariah spoke of Israel's hard-hearted state, the cause of their exile, when he said, "They made their hearts diamond-hard lest they should hear the law and the words that the LORD of hosts had sent by his Spirit through the former prophets. Therefore great anger came from the LORD of hosts" (Zech. 7:12). Again and again, the reason why people did not hear God's Word was because of sin, which resulted in condemnation.

New Testament passages

This theme of condemnation does not end with the Old Testament. In fact, because God's revelation became clearer and brighter with Jesus's coming, the condemnation is more severe in the New Testament. Throughout Jesus's ministry he called for people to respond to his teaching, saying, "He who has ears to hear, let him hear" (Matt. 11:15). This was his way of distinguishing those who were spiritually illumined to hear God's Word from those who were not. Many have wondered why, when Jesus taught parables, most of his hearers did not have the first clue what he was talking about. Why did Jesus so often teach this way? Was he trying to make spiritual truths easier to understand through stories? If so, why did so many people either miss or reject the point? Jesus's parables were not merely teaching tools, however, but also served as a condemnation of those who were spiritually blind. In this way, the parables were exclusively received by those who were illumined to understand them. Jesus actually summarized his parabolic ministry by looking back to Isaiah's commission and showing a similar focus. The Son of God saw himself as picking up where Isaiah had left off:

This is why I speak to them in parables, because seeing they do not see, and hearing they do not hear, nor do they understand. Indeed, in their case the prophecy of Isaiah is fulfilled that says:

"You will indeed hear but never understand,
  and you will indeed see but never perceive.
For this people's heart has grown dull,
  and with their ears they can barely hear,
  and their eyes they have closed,
lest they should see with their eyes
  and hear with their ears
and understand with their heart
  and turn, and I would heal them."

But blessed are your eyes, for they see, and your ears, for they hear. For truly, I say to you, many prophets and righteous people longed to see what you see, and did not see it, and to hear what you hear, and did not hear it.   (Matt. 13:13–17)

This could seem confusing. Why would people understand the basic point or moral of a parable and yet still not believe in Jesus? Jesus's parables were not obscure. Unbelievers approach parables in a way similar to reading well-known fables, while the illumined person moves beyond the superficial clarity of parables to the actual meaning and deeper implications. Jonathan Edwards, the notable 18th-century preacher, helps to clarify this:

It is possible that a man might know how to interpret all the types, parables, enigmas, and allegories in the Bible, and not have one beam of spiritual light in his mind; because he may not have the least degree of that spiritual sense of the holy beauty of divine things which has been spoken of, and may see nothing of this kind of glory in anything contained in any of these mysteries, or any other part of the Scripture.[1]

Edwards is saying that illumination—sensing the Lord's "holy beauty"— is distinct from simple interpretation. This is an important distinction to make when thinking about what Jesus really meant about "seeing" and "hearing" truth. As stated at the beginning of this work, whether or not a person is illumined is truly a matter of spiritual life and death.

Perhaps one of the saddest examples of this comes from a story the Lord told in Luke 16:19–31. This is the account of the rich man and Lazarus, which many understand to be a parable. This story reads like one of Jesus's parables, but Jesus uses real names, which seems to indicate real people in a real historical setting. Jesus never used names in any of his parables. Either way, this is perhaps one of the most sobering stories in the Bible. Jesus told of two men:

There was a rich man who was clothed in purple and fine linen and who feasted sumptuously every day. And at his gate was laid a poor man named Lazarus, covered with sores, who desired to be fed with what fell from the rich man's table. Moreover, even the dogs came and licked his sores. The poor man died and was carried by the angels to Abraham's side. The rich man also died and was buried, and in Hades, being in torment, he lifted up his eyes and saw Abraham far off and Lazarus at his side. And he called out, "Father Abraham, have mercy on me, and send Lazarus to dip the end of his finger in water and cool my tongue, for I am in anguish in this flame." But Abraham said, "Child, remember that you in your lifetime received your good things, and Lazarus in like manner bad things; but now he is comforted here, and you are in anguish. And besides all this, between us and you a great chasm has been fixed, in order that those who would pass from here to you may not be able, and none may cross from there to us." And he said, "Then I beg you, father, to send him to my father's house—

for I have five brothers—so that he may warn them, lest they also come into this place of torment." But Abraham said, "They have Moses and the Prophets; let them hear them." And he said, "No, father Abraham, but if someone goes to them from the dead, they will repent." He said to him, "If they do not hear Moses and the Prophets, neither will they be convinced if someone should rise from the dead."   (Luke 16:19–31)

Much could be said about this passage, but note how the rich man begs that Lazarus be sent back to warn his five brothers, keeping them from suffering eternal hell as he is (Luke 16:27–28). The Lord's response is amazing. Abraham, understood here to be the Lord, says, "They have Moses and the Prophets; let them hear them" (Luke 16:29). The Lord is not so much rebuking the rich man as affirming the transforming power of the Word of God. The rich man, missing the point, makes the case that, though his brothers might ignore the Word, they would surely repent if they encountered a miraculous resurrected messenger sent specifically to them (Luke 16:30). Abraham's final statement to the rich man reveals the true nature of what it means to be under this condemnation. He says, "If they do not hear Moses and the Prophets, neither will they be convinced if someone should rise from the dead" (Luke 16:31). No amount of sensationalism will change a heart that is rejecting the light. A person who will not see spiritual light from the Word will not see God's glorious light displayed in miracles.

This is like the state of so many eyewitnesses of Jesus's miraculous signs. They remained cynical, not willing to fully embrace Jesus as God. Jesus performed miracles to reveal himself as God, but he was not naïve regarding the fickle nature of most who followed him. Scripture documents Jesus's response, stating that he "did not entrust himself to them, because he knew all people" (John 2:24). They did not give themselves to Jesus, and Jesus did not give himself to them. The crowds were not illumined, but condemned.

Jesus's words in John's Gospel further confirm this sobering reality. For most Christians, John 3:16 is the quintessential call to believe and receive eternal life, but people often forget what Jesus said in verse 18. Though Jesus guaranteed eternal life for all who believe, he also stated what is equally true—those who do not believe are "condemned already." They are presently in a state of condemnation which may end up as eternal condemnation without the Lord. Jesus described people in this state as those who reject light because light exposes their moral darkness (John 3:19–20). This is the sad plight for people presently condemned—they want their sin, which is killing and dooming them, yet they need Jesus's rescue.

This kind of talk does not stop with Jesus. The book of Acts picks it right up with the account of Stephen, a man known by the early church to be "full of faith and of the Holy Spirit" (6:5). Stephen's tenacity was sure to cause friction with unbelievers. From the record in Acts, it seems that very soon after he was affirmed for church leadership he was falsely accused of being a troublemaker by those in the synagogue with whom he "disputed." He found himself having to testify before a hostile tribunal with his life on the line (Acts 6:9–7:1). Stephen's sermon pulled no punches. He ended up condemning his hearers as blind men, much as Isaiah and Jesus did.

His descriptions were meant to sting. He said, "You stiff-necked people, uncircumcised in heart and ears, you always resist the Holy Spirit. As your fathers did, so do you" (Acts 7:51). His audience did not appreciate his assessment of them. Their angry response makes this obvious: "But they cried out with a loud voice and stopped their ears and rushed together at him" (Acts 7:57). Luke, the descriptive and detailed author of Acts, points out that they plugged their ears—a physical expression of outright rejection of the truth. This hardness of heart turned murderous—they attacked and killed Stephen (Acts 7:58). Persecution of this kind is very foreign to Western believers today, but a way to experience a small dose is to tell people that Jesus is the only way to heaven, that their sin has offended a holy God, and that unless they repent of it they will suffer a deserved punishment in hell forever. This might give a small taste of what Stephen experienced. Also, God might choose to open hearts to the gospel through this witness.

Throughout the book of Acts the early church grew by leaps and bounds by means of gospel preaching. This same preaching was part of the ministry of condemnation. Paul's summary of his ministry, which serves as a postscript to Acts, contains a direct reference to Isaiah 6 and places Paul's ministry in the same preaching lineage. First Isaiah, then Jesus, and now

Paul were all rejected by God's chosen people. Quoting Isaiah 6:9, Paul put himself right in this stream of rejection, saying,

The Holy Spirit was right in saying to your fathers through Isaiah the prophet:
"Go to this people, and say, 'You will indeed hear but never understand,
   and you will indeed see but never perceive.
For this people's heart has grown dull,
   and with their ears they can barely hear,
   and their eyes they have closed;
lest they should see with their eyes
   and hear with their ears
and understand with their heart
   and turn, and I would heal them.'" (Acts 28:25–27)

Paul went on to expand this theme in his New Testament epistles. In his letter to the Romans he referred to the Jews' present blind state, saying, "God gave them a spirit of stupor, eyes that would not see and ears that would not hear, down to this very day" (Rom. 11:8). It is interesting to note that Paul did not stop with the Jews but also exhorted one of his most beloved New Testament churches along these same lines. In 2 Thessalonians, Paul warned the church not to fall into deception regarding the timing of the Day of the Lord. He specifically marked the end times by the coming of "the man of lawlessness," who is the Anti-Christ (2 Thes. 2:3). Paul wrote that many in the end would be deceived by this man, and characterized that man's leadership as "the activity of Satan" (2:9). It is interesting to note that, just as in 2 Corinthians 4:1–4, Satan is here seen as the agent of deception. Paul spoke of people as being in a state of "perishing" because of their sin, and refusing "to love the truth" (2:10). They are then ultimately "condemned" (2:12): "Therefore God sends them a strong delusion, so that they may believe what is false, in order that all may be condemned who did not believe the truth but had pleasure in unrighteousness."

In Ephesians Paul condemned Gentile blindness, saying that the Gentiles "... are darkened in their understanding ... due to their hardness of heart" (Eph. 4:18). He then picked on the false teachers in the church, pointing out that they were "… never able to arrive at a knowledge of the truth" (2 Tim. 3:7). Paul had the same result from preaching that Jesus did. For some, his ministry was a savor of life to life, but for others it was death to death (2 Cor. 2:16).

Look at the book of Hebrews, an epistle filled with warnings. Here is written what is perhaps the most frightening and sobering condemnation of gospel-rejecters in the entire Bible: "For it is impossible, in the case of those who have once been enlightened, who have tasted the heavenly gift, and have shared in the Holy Spirit, and have tasted the goodness of the word of God and the powers of the age to come, and then have fallen away, to restore them again to repentance" (Heb. 6:4–6). Out of all the passages on spiritual blindness in the New Testament, this is probably the most stinging, and also the most applicable to today's church. These verses rebuke anybody who would dare to play church or fake Christianity. This section describes self-professed believers who have experienced a superficial repentance and have been enlightened in a merely external sense. These superficial experiences have come from tasting spiritual realities—the "believers" have been enjoying the benefits of God that come to his people and have been seeing his power all around them. They have been exposed to answered prayers, powerful preaching, powerful worship, counsel, sacrificial love, and much more, all while never really letting go of their love for sin and never really giving themselves to Jesus. They have just enough light from the Holy Spirit to experience God's power, yet they still turn their backs on the truth of the gospel, spurning Jesus Christ. The Bible is here warning that rejecting Christ after being exposed at this level to God's revelation renders people beyond reach—they are condemned.

Church-history examples

John Owen, the 17th-century Puritan pastor, theologian, and statesman from London, wrote about what he called a "two stage illumination." Owen wrote that the doctrine of illumination encompassed "all the light or knowledge we have of spiritual things"[2] for both superficial and saving levels. He surmised that the mere exposure to truth will affect a person's soul, although this stage will not be saving or regenerating. He called this unregenerate person's faith "mere natural reason ... being only a naked assent to the doctrines revealed."[3] Owen derived this teaching in part from Jesus's parable of the soils, and spoke of those "who, when they hear the word, receive it with joy. But these have no root ... and ... fall away" (Luke 8:13). Owen wrote of this pre-saving light, "[There is first] a disquieting sense of the guilt of sin, with respect to the law, threatenings, and judgments of God ... Sorrow or grief for sin committed because past and irrecoverable, which is the formal reason of the condemning or legal sorrow (cf. 2 Cor. 7:10 "worldly grief produces death") which brings men into bondage under fear."[4] He understood that, no matter how much light there is, "... many sit all their days under the preaching of the Gospel, and feel none of these effects."[5]

Jonathan Edwards understood this balance, calling superficial illumination or pre-illumination "common illuminations." He wrote, "... men's religious affections truly arise from some instruction or light in the understanding ... [but that] affection is not gracious unless the light which is the ground of it be spiritual."[6] Like Owen, Edwards wrote of the working out of "common illuminations," in which the initial response seems genuine but the faith eventually dissipates: "Many ... have had mighty strong affections at first conversion, afterwards become dry, and wither, and consume, and pine, and die away: and now their hypocrisy is manifest; if not to all the world by open profaneness."[7] This kind of faith that falls away could be called "demon faith," where people superficially "... believe to be true what the Scriptures testify ... [that which] is known also to the devils and many of the lost."[8]

Implications for the preacher

These passages show that at the core people are spiritually blind and deaf to God's Word because of sin. Sin acts as a fog, clouding man's ability to perceive the gospel's glory and truthfulness, and turning a person's heart away from God toward Satan's kingdom and the things of the world. Satan operates in tandem with man's own sin, covering the eyes of unbelievers to keep them from seeing Jesus's shining face (2 Cor. 4:4).

The disconnect between unbelievers and truth is neither on a cognitive level, nor is it based upon their mental inability to grasp spiritual truths.

Instead, the truth simply comes across "to their unregenerate judgment [as] ... 'foolishness' or nonsense to their unredeemed minds."[9] As one homiletics scholar put it, "Facts inform but only the Spirit transforms, and that is what is missing when the Spirit's illumination is not present."[10] The Bible offers hope, for although this first stage of illumination can be rejected, it can also serve as what Owen called "preparatory operations on the souls of men."[11] Under this first stage Owen admitted, "Many are thus enlightened, and yet never converted," but this light can be "in order of nature ... previous to conversion, and ... materially preparatory to [conversion] ... for saving grace enters into the soul by light ... therefore, a gift of God."[12] He knew that "... the word preached is the instrumental cause" for genuine conversion to take place.[13]

Understanding what God's Word says about the condemnation that occurs because of gospel proclamation is important in shaping the preacher's biblical expectations for his preaching. The preacher does not really know God's goals when he communicates truth, since God's will regarding each and every ministry is secret (see Deut. 29:29). It may seem that God is using his Word as a tool to judge condemned sinners more often than to convert them. This concept can be discouraging. It might cause a heart to feel defeated and say, "Why even bother to study God's Word? Why prepare expository sermons when most of the people who hear me will never change?"

Instead of thinking that, think about this: The pressure actually disappears with the realization that life-change for the hearer is not won and lost by the preacher's performance. How well he communicates is not the determining factor as to whether or not people spiritually grasp truth. This does not mean there is a free pass to become a lazy Bible student or sloppy communicator. On the contrary, knowing that illumination is God's work frees the preacher to focus on preaching with clarity as opposed to focusing on style or relevance. Practically, this leads to great freedom in the pulpit, since the preacher's heart is focused on being faithful, handling the truth with integrity, and trusting God with the results—regardless of whether God chooses to convict or condemn, bring spiritual life or death, wound or heal. Whatever the result, the Lord gets glory (2 Cor. 2:15–16).

Paul's firm grasp on this concept made him unflappable in his preaching ministry, and able to say "we do not lose heart" (2 Cor. 4:1). He stayed the course and did not become a manipulator of people's emotions but remained a faithful communicator of truth, leaving the results to God (2 Cor. 4:2). Calvin's persevering and powerful testimony also came from understanding this. Calvin well understood both the source of spiritual blindness and its remedy, illumination. He documented this, saying,

Our mind is too rude to be able to comprehend the spiritual wisdom of God which is revealed to us by faith, and our hearts are too prone either to diffidence or to a perverse confidence in ourselves or creatures, to rest in God of their own accord. But the Holy Spirit by his illumination makes us capable of understanding those things which would otherwise far exceed our capacity, and forms us to a firm persuasion, by sealing the promises of salvation on our hearts.[14]

It is a sobering reality that people are condemned by their sin; however, God's Word provides the remedy. The Lord has provided the means for the lights to be turned on—simply by allowing people to hear the truth. From the very beginning God has illumined communicators of his Word so that they will preach and hearers will be illumined.

Notes

1 **Jonathan Edwards,** *The Religious Affections* (1746; 1986, Carlisle, PA: Banner of Truth), p. 204.

2 **John Owen,** *The Holy Spirit: His Gifts and Power* (Grand Rapids, MI: Kregel, 1954), p. 138.

3 Ibid. p. 138.

4 Ibid. p. 137.

5 Ibid. p. 140.

6 **Edwards,** *The Religious Affections*, p. 195.

7 Ibid. p. 193, n.

8 **B. B. Warfield,** *Calvin and Augustine* (1956; 1980, Philadelphia: Presbyterian and Reformed, 1980), p. 77, n.

9 **Greg Heisler,** *Spirit-Led Preaching: The Holy Spirit's Role in Sermon Preparation and Delivery* (Nashville: B & H Academic, 2007), p. 46.

10 Ibid.

11 Owen, *The Holy Spirit*, p. 135.

12 Ibid. p. 38.

13 Ibid. p. 137.

14 John Calvin, trans. **Henry Beveridge,** *Tracts and Treatises on the Doctrine and Worship of the Church* (1849; 1958, Grand Rapids, MI: Eerdmans, 1958), 2:53.

Communication for illumination

How is God's Word meant to bring about change? Think about this: The most monumental physical change that ever took place began with God speaking—he spoke creation into existence. God said, "'Let there be light,' and there was light" (Gen. 1:3). These simple words from God are the genesis of everything anyone who has ever lived has ever seen or felt. Likewise, God's revealed Word brings about monumental spiritual change. His Word transforms lives blinded by Satan and lost in sin, changing them into believers who love the glory of Christ Jesus.

Perhaps one of the most fundamental validations that the Lord works through his Word is that the New Testament demands that qualified men preach the Word to effect change (2 Tim. 4:1–2). Though preaching is still being carried out in various forms and fashions in the church today, there are new preaching philosophies and methods that ignore and undermine its biblically defined purpose. The primary goal for the preacher is that the Spirit of God would illumine God's Word in the hearts of the hearers, but some current preaching trends don't seem to agree with this.

A disregard for illumination

Doug Pagitt has written a highly sought-after book on preaching in today's culture. Entitled *Preaching Re-Imagined: The Role of the Sermon in Communities of Faith*, this book promotes a new method of communication which usurps biblical preaching and at its core completely ignores the vital connection between the Holy Spirit and the Word of God. Pagitt is the pastor of Solomon's Porch, a church intentionally known as cutting edge and contemporary and which, as its mission, seeks to reach postmoderns in Minneapolis. He also serves as part of a network called Emergent, which is comprised of self-termed postmodern Christian leaders. These leaders are focused on what they believe the church is becoming based on the way our society currently thinks. The movement attempts to introduce a new way to communicate and to reach out within its sphere of influence.

Pagitt's book is his plea for a new method of preaching. He argues that the traditional method of preaching, which he calls "speaching," is ineffective and passé. This view holds that the monologue method, whereby a listening congregation hears truth declared, undercuts the listener's opportunity to contribute and, worse yet, is born of pastors who are enamored with control and want to dictate the conclusions taught and applied.

Pagitt asserts that it is time to move on to a relationally interactive preaching style which he has named "Progressive Dialogue."[1] This he defines as preaching whereby "the content of the presentation is established in the context of healthy relationship between the presenter and the listeners, and substantive changes in the content are then created as a result of this relationship."[2] He makes the argument that the method of delivery is not the core issue. The core issue is really a matter of who possesses the sermon content and where it comes from. Paggit's simple answer is that it comes from both "teller and the hearers."[3]

Pagitt spends the entire first half of his book reasoning why one should not preach in monologue but rather in Progressive Dialogue. The most outrageous reason he gives to stop "speaching" is that "it doesn't work."[4] People who have their own perspectives on truth are never given the chance "… to engage the preacher, to offer up [their] viewpoint, to engage in discussion."[5] Under "speaching," he argues, people are dehumanized and not viewed as participating in the priesthood of believers. The traditional lecture format "… cultivates a sense in which the pastor is admired, unquestioned, and isolated."[6] Pagitt argues that control and authority should be taken out of the hands of the preacher and given to the listening community. The listeners are the ones who dictate, through open discussion, the outcome of each sermon and the personal implications therein.

Pagitt uses biblical narratives as support for Progressive Dialogue. He cites passages like Luke 24, where Jesus dialogued about truth with the two on the road to Emmaus, and Acts 10, where Peter came to a clearer understanding of truth through the process of talking with Cornelius. He also sees Paul's epistles as simple correspondence (which he calls dialogue) between Paul and the churches.

The final section of his book is basically a "how to." He covers everything from the preacher's tone of voice, the church facility (actual set-up of meeting area), to the role of the Bible in Progressive Dialogue. A noticeable hole in Pagitt's book is that he leaves no room for traditional preaching. At the end of his book, he essentially capstones all he has said with the statement that Progressive Dialogue is "A New Approach for a New Age."7

Perhaps his past experience as a youth speaker has some bearing on his passion for this new method. He speaks of suffering guilt over past manipulation of youth campers. He seems to view modern mega-church speakers as manipulators, based upon his own experience. Reacting against this past or not, Pagitt is drawn toward a relational method that he believes to be more authentic. Progressive Dialogue "… implies that the pastor must have intimate relationships with the community instead of being a stranger on stage, an ethic Pagitt terms deep ecclesiology."8

Interactive dialogical teaching is not by nature evil. It is often used in both secular and Christian arenas. The problem arises when the Word of God is relegated to the role of active participant when it is by rights the authority before which everyone should bow. Pagitt writes,

The Bible is really good at speaking for herself, but there are times when the other persons in the dialogue don't know enough about the context and situation to make sense of what they hear. It's during those points when I insert myself into the conversation to offer clarification. Then there are times when the Bible is finished talking, and it becomes my time to share my take on it.9

This version of Progressive Dialogue looks like liberal neo-orthodoxy in postmodern dress. Neo-orthodoxy is famous for its discussions in which the Bible becomes the Word of God as it is discussed. It takes on significance as people ask, "What does this passage mean to me?" Pagitt attempts to remove this likeness by defining "truth" as different from "The Truth."10 He defines "truth" as reality and how a person perceives reality, and "The Truth" seems to be Scripture. Defining "truth" in this way puts the perspectives of everyone—whether preachers or hearers—on a par. It does away with objective doctrine, placing everyone's experience above "The Truth." This looks a lot like neo-orthodoxy.

Pagitt's approach must not be considered only on a methodological basis, as it was by one reviewer who wrote,

Pagitt's analysis of the education model at the heart of so much contemporary congregational practice is perceptive but, sadly, undertheorized. It is perceptive because it offers an insightful postmodern challenge to one of the most sacred cornerstones of the Christendom church: that knowledge gained through a largely passive education process will somehow lead to active behavior change.[11]

This reviewer, like Pagitt, assumes that traditional preaching is "passive education." This perspective completely ignores the power that is inherent in the Word of God (2 Tim. 3:16) and the significance of the priesthood of the believer (1 Peter 2:9), whereby he or she is spiritually gifted to apprehend truth as it is preached.

Pagitt refers to D. Martyn Lloyd-Jones's *Preachers and Preaching*, speaking of how he is diametrically opposed to Lloyd-Jones's form and philosophy of preaching. During the 1970s, Lloyd-Jones addressed the new response-oriented additions to church worship, saying these were, at best, secondary to preaching, and, at worst, simply entertainment methods which marked the decline of strong preaching.[12] Pagitt is clear that Lloyd-Jones's preaching method "… bears little resemblance [to his],"[13] and he jokingly concludes the discussion by suggesting that those who side with Lloyd-Jones focus on "refining" that preaching method instead of "spending time in [Pagitt's] … book" and that "this might be the time to exercise your right to the publisher's money-back guarantee."[14] He views it all as just a difference of opinion.

What, however, is dangerous about Pagitt's book is that it does not respect the authority, power, or clarity inherent in the Word of God. Monologue preachers are characterized as power-hungry, but as one reviewer says,

A biblical view invests authority in the Word itself and not in the preacher. Biblical preachers understand that the power is not in the opinions of the preacher but in the revelation of God's activity, character and will as it is offered in the Bible. Authority, then, resides neither in the community nor in the speacher. Authority comes from God.[15]

The Bible testifies to its clarity (Ps. 119:130); consequently, the preacher can, with great confidence, explain it to his people. Pagitt muddies this truth by casting the monologue approach aside when he says of preachers that "[by offering] … simplified explanations for something that scholars and theologians have wrestled with for centuries, we not only strip people of the ability to read the Bible with … confidence but we strip the Bible of her richness and beauty."[16] But is not the richness and beauty of God's Word rooted in the fact that God has spoken authoritatively and clearly, and that he enables people to understand what he has said?

One very disconcerting statement comes near the end of the book. Pagitt crosses a line theologically by pitting propositional truth against the ministry of Christ. He cites Mark 1:15, where Jesus's public ministry is summarized by this declaration: "The time is fulfilled, and the kingdom of God is at hand; repent and believe in the gospel." Pagitt writes,

After reading this … I started wondering. What was the Good News [gospel] Jesus was referring to all those years before his death, burial, and resurrection? Could it be that the Good News Jesus talked about was less a call to believe in the things that happened to him or would happen to and through him than an invitation into Kingdom life?[17]

With this rhetorical question he is undermining the very heart of the doctrine of soteriology. Jesus is calling for repentance and offering eternal life, not inviting people into a "Christian lifestyle." Errors such as these are to be expected whenever a person elevates methodology above the Word and the power of the Holy Spirit.[18]

As One Without Authority by Dr. Fred B. Craddock[19] is another influential book on new preaching trends. Dr. Craddock is credentialed as Bandy Emeritus Professor of Preaching and New Testament in the Candler School of Theology, Emory University in Atlanta, Georgia. He is an ordained minister and lectures in theological ivy-league schools. He has authored many books, but none so prophetic concerning the postmodern pulpit as this. This short book puts forth the New Homiletic that has been shaping the landscape of preachers and preaching for the last several decades.

What is disconcerting is that there is no emphasis on the transforming power of the Word, just as with Pagitt's book. In the first two chapters Craddock lays out his foundational material explaining how to study and preach. He makes the case that it is a must for the preacher to stay current with today's television-conditioned listeners. Gone are the days of the authoritarian three-point preachers. Today's preacher must be a blend of college professor and great story-teller. For the pulpit to come out of the shadows and into the spotlight, a preacher's sermons must engage hearers in a journey in which questions are raised but conclusions are to be drawn individually by the hearers, by implication only. The sermon is to be fluid, and must sound like—or actually be—a conversation.

Craddock believes it is necessary to call for a marked shift from what he calls "deductive preaching" to "inductive preaching." He sees deductive preaching as the old-school style, in which an authoritarian preacher takes what he has learned from his Bible study and transforms it into a sequential outline filled with wide-sweeping conclusions and applications. According to Craddock, this is unacceptable as it creates a complete disconnect between the particular genre of the text preached and the experience of those listening. The inductive method challenges the preacher not to *teach* the text but rather to *experience* it, and to take his hearers along for the ride.

Craddock wants the preacher's method of presentation to fit the content and genre of each particular text. He must decide whose perspective he will teach from—that of the original Bible author or of the original Bible hearer. Then comes what Craddock calls "incarnating the Word," by which he means that the preacher must somehow capture how he is stirred by the questions raised during personal study and pattern the delivery in terms of this experience. One journal review summarizes Craddock's preaching model this way: "... communication is less formal, more dialogical, more conversational—and ... the preacher must expose himself/herself to the 'speaking situation.' The preacher should open his faith struggle to the hearers. It is preaching in an incarnational mold."[20]

The method here borders on neo-orthodoxy, the same concern raised about Pagitt's book. Because Craddock emphasizes oral tradition, focusing on the significance and beauty of language, he presents preaching more as an event than simple Bible declaration and explanation. He raises questions about exactly when the Bible becomes the Word of God, asking, "… whether this method [his new homiletic] makes the Word of God dependent on the listener [and also,] since the inductive method places so much responsibility on the ear of the hearer, does not this imply that the Word is the Word only when it is heard?"[21]

Another emphasis is on the use of the imagination in preaching; he believes a sermon must be told as a unified story under a single point. The example sermons in his appendix read as well-written short stories. They are innocuous and without authority. His book is about getting results. He desperately wants people to experience a sermon. An emphasis on experience, in and of itself, is not necessarily wrong unless—as is Craddock's idea—the experience eclipses the preacher's mandate to reprove, rebuke, exhort, read, preach, explain, and apply the Scriptures (see 1 Tim. 4:13; 2 Tim. 3:16–4:2).

Though he cites Jesus's parabolic teaching style and Paul's writing style as examples for communication, Craddock simply misses the point of preaching altogether. At its heart, preaching cannot be listener-based. Even reviewers sympathetic to his view see the dangers inherent in this method. One reviewer writes, "[Craddock's] … concern for the listener makes for more effective preaching but it also has got him into some difficulty at times with evangelicals who would question his fidelity to the text of Scripture … Craddock struggles with a tension between exegetical faithfulness and inductive movement."[22]

To qualify: If Craddock's emphases are taken as secondary in the formulation of preaching, they are not all bad, and (in terms of speaking style) can even perhaps be helpful. For instance, sermons should be studied, shaped, and preached according to the genre of the particular biblical text. The preaching outline should inductively rise from the text. Preaching can and often should be conversational and non-threatening. This way the preacher hides behind the Word of God. It is crucial for the preacher to think through creative ways to draw a clear connection between the text preached and the people hearing it. Use of imagination is a God-given gift, and it is a mistake not to use it. Also, the unifying theme should be found in each particular text preached;[23] otherwise, preaching is merely running commentary with little or no cohesion or impact. A sermon should tell a story—the story found in the biblical and historical context of any given passage—and it ought to draw hearers back into the original setting and the implications therein. Regarding application, it ought to be unforced and not moralistic. The hearer must be taking the truth to heart, applying Scripture according to his or her own set of circumstances as the Spirit of God illumines the mind.

What, however, is dangerous about Craddock's book is that it is devoid of a call to teach the Bible—God's change-agent. This reviewer unintentionally makes my point:

Times have changed … the book was written in a period when a preacher could in many neighborhoods presuppose a considerable familiarity with the Bible and the key theological tenets of the tradition. Sad to say, all that has for the most part passed away … It is probably time for a *new* new homiletic that will help preachers address our suddenly post-Christian world.[24]

The problem is that the very reason why people are so biblically ignorant is because a great deal of preaching is largely about experience, with minimal to no biblical content.

Craddock is insistent that preaching should create dialogue. He claims that the key for today's preaching is something he calls "deep resonances,"[25] whereby preaching is simply connecting with people's memories, their past experiences. The preacher should bring up something that resonates with people, creating a dialogue, which is the key to preaching. Craddock finds this concept in ancient art, philosophy, and throughout the Bible, which he speaks of as being "layered,"[26] meaning that the Bible repeats stories in order to bring up that past experience and connect with the reader. The conclusion is left open-ended so that people will essentially finish the sermon for themselves.

Thinking through preaching technique is not wrong or sinful, and in terms of preaching style it can often be helpful. The problem with the approach taken by trendsetters Doug Pagitt and Fred Craddock is that their contributions to preaching completely ignore the essential doctrine of illumination, especially as it concerns communicating God's Word. Ignoring what is so fundamental misses the essence of preaching. With style at the center of today's hottest preaching discussions, the fear is that church pulpits will starve the flock rather than feed it.

Illumined to communicate

What, then, does God's Word teach about preaching? A survey of the Word shows how foundational the doctrine of illumination is to biblical communication. The Bible emphasizes not only illumined communication but also illumined communicators. In the earliest biblical record God is seen strategically speaking to patriarchs such as Noah, Abraham, Isaac, Jacob, Joseph, and Moses. When these men heard the LORD's communication, they became God's spokesmen.

Old and New Testament prophets received direct revelation from God. This differs from preachers, who communicate from the revelation that has already been given. However, there remains significant overlap in how the Holy Spirit illumines the minds of both prophets and preachers on the basis of revelation.

God's interaction with Joseph gives a clear example of how God turned men into his mouthpieces. As the story goes, Joseph had been imprisoned by Pharaoh due to false accusations, and then through a series of God-planned circumstances he was recommended by Pharaoh's chief cupbearer to interpret a symbolic dream (Gen. 39–41). Because none of Pharaoh's magicians or wise men could interpret the dream and Joseph could, Pharaoh said, "Can we find a man like this, in whom is the Spirit of God?" Then Pharaoh said to Joseph, "Since God has shown you all this, there is none so discerning and wise as you are" (Gen. 41:38–39). The implication from the text is that Joseph was spiritually illumined to communicate God's will to Pharaoh. It is illumination that produces the very things for which Joseph was commended: *discernment* and *wisdom*.

After the time of the patriarchs, God raised up kings to lead his people. These men possessed the massive responsibilities of speaking for God and ruling his people, tasks which carried with them the expectation that the kings would possess spiritual discernment. What is notable is the means by which the kings were instructed to acquire this. The Old Testament Law required them to carefully read the Law, God's Word, and then to write a word-for-word copy of it.

This command can be found in the book of Deuteronomy: "And when he sits on the throne of his kingdom, he shall write for himself in a book a copy of this law, approved by the Levitical priests" (Deut. 17:18). The king needed to "read in it all the days of his life," with the result that he would "learn to fear the LORD his God by keeping all the words of this law and these statutes, and doing them" (Deut.17:19). This exercise gave recognition to the fact that in a very real sense this revelation was just as authentic and powerful for each succeeding generation as when the Pentateuch was first written. For the king, it would be almost as if God were speaking audibly to him. Though spiritual illumination is not directly mentioned, the clear implication is that the king's fear of the LORD would come from spiritual illumination (see 2 Sam. 23:1–3; Prov. 1:7; Isa. 11:2–4; Micah 6:9; Acts 13:26; 2 Cor. 7:1; Heb. 4:1).

Don't miss the serious connection between the king and the Scripture. The king was entrusted with the weighty responsibility of ruling over the LORD's nation. Throughout his lifetime he would make significant decisions in regard to the physical and spiritual well-being of his people. What was the prescribed key to success? He needed to be illumined by God's law to fear the LORD.

Spiritual illumination was essential in order for the king to reign with success over Israel. Look at what the prophet Samuel said to Israel's first king, Saul. Samuel prophesied that "... the Spirit of the LORD will rush upon you, and you will prophesy with them and be turned into another man" (1 Sam. 10:6). Because of Saul's wicked character his illumination was superficial and temporary. He ultimately turned away from God, yet as king he possessed for a time the ability to prophesy and communicate for God. In the early days, spiritual communication marked Saul's rule (1 Sam. 19:24), but his character eventually caused him to lose his kingship.

Saul's successor was David, a man with godly character who was illumined to communicate God's truth to the end of his life. In 2 Samuel there is a significant epitaph regarding David's life and ministry that testifies to this:

Now these are the last words of David:
The oracle of David, the son of Jesse,
the oracle of the man who was raised on high,
the anointed of the God of Jacob,
the sweet psalmist of Israel:
"The Spirit of the LORD speaks by me;
    his word is on my tongue.
The God of Israel has spoken;
    the Rock of Israel has said to me:
When one rules justly over men,
    ruling in the fear of God ..."   (2 Sam. 23:1–3)

No other time in David's life better demonstrates David's passion for spiritual illumination than when he thought he had lost it. He knew that possessing this gift from God was a high privilege and essential for him as king of Israel. When he was immoral with Bathsheba and followed that with a massive cover-up scandal (2 Sam. 11:2–21), he knew he was in serious danger of having his gift stripped away by the LORD. He eventually repented of his sin, and what stands out here is the significant emphasis he placed on begging the LORD that he might not lose spiritual illumination. He prayed, "Cast me not away from your presence, and take not your Holy Spirit from me" (Ps. 51:11). By asking that God would not take the Holy Spirit from him he was not trying to protect his eternal salvation. This was not David's struggle. Rather, he was asking God that he be allowed to maintain a rule empowered by the Spirit even though he had committed adultery and orchestrated Uriah's murder, acts that were both punishable by death. Amazingly, God honored this request by not only granting him forgiveness but also allowing David to continue as king. Psalm 32 attests to this.

It is fitting that David's son Solomon, next in line to the throne, prayed for this same spiritual discernment. God honored his wise request as he did with David, and 1 Kings 4:29 documents this, saying, "... God gave

Solomon wisdom and understanding beyond measure, and breadth of mind like the sand on the seashore." Solomon had the reputation among the nations in his day of being the wisest man who had ever lived. It is only fitting that he authored the majority of the Bible's wisdom literature—the Song of Solomon, much of Proverbs, as well as the book of Ecclesiastes, which is, in effect, a twelve-chapter sermon delivered by "the Preacher," the "the son of David" (Eccles. 1:1).

Though he was simply a frail human being, King David foreshadowed the Messiah, the one who was to come, the ultimate King and the one who came as the ultimate Spirit-anointed communicator. The prophet Isaiah characterized Christ and his ministry as illumined by the Spirit when he said,

There shall come forth a shoot from the stump of Jesse,
    and a branch from his roots shall bear fruit.
And the Spirit of the LORD shall rest upon him,
    the Spirit of wisdom and understanding,
    the Spirit of counsel and might,
    the Spirit of knowledge and the fear of the LORD.   (Isa. 11:1–2)

The Gospels confirm that Isaiah's prophecy came true. Jesus came and bannered his entire earthly ministry by quoting Isaiah 61:1 (see Luke 4:18). In the synagogue he read Isaiah with reference to himself, saying,

The Spirit of the Lord GOD is upon me,
    because the LORD has anointed me
to bring good news to the poor;
    he has sent me to bind up the brokenhearted,
to proclaim liberty to the captives,
    and the opening of the prison to those who are bound ...   (Isa. 61:1)

Because Jesus is God, it might seem that Jesus did not need the Holy Spirit when he preached. However, he still made the clear connection between the Holy Spirit's anointing and his role as gospel communicator. Though Jesus, as both God and man, was the quintessential communicator, he came in the tradition of the rest of the prophets—Jeremiah, Ezekiel, Daniel, and all the others anointed to speak for God. We know that the Lord Jesus knew preaching to be his mandate, not only because he characterized his ministry under the banner of Isaiah 61:1, but also because of the statement he made just on the heels of this, when he said, "I must preach the good news of the kingdom of God to the other towns as well; for I was sent for this purpose" (Luke 4:43). Jesus fulfilled this preaching ministry, and those who followed in his steps likewise became examples of illumined communicators.

Luke told in his Gospel of the godly man Simeon who spent his life waiting in the temple for Jesus the Messiah to be born. In his account of Simeon's experience when Christ was first presented at the temple, Luke emphasized the dawning of the new spiritual day. Luke wrote,

> Now there was a man in Jerusalem, whose name was Simeon, and this man was righteous and devout, waiting for the consolation of Israel, and the Holy Spirit was upon him. And it had been revealed to him by the Holy Spirit that he would not see death before he had seen the Lord's Christ. And he came in the Spirit into the temple, and when the parents brought in the child Jesus, to do for him according to the custom of the Law, he took him up in his arms and blessed God and said, "Lord, now you are letting your servant depart in peace, according to your word; for my eyes have seen your salvation that you have prepared in the presence of all peoples, a light for revelation to the Gentiles, and for glory to your people Israel." (Luke 2:25–32)

What is fascinating here is how the Spirit of God illumined Simeon to know of and recognize the Messiah and then to proclaim that Christ was the light for revelation, or the illumination, to the Gentiles. Christ's ministry, in a functional sense, can be boiled down to anointed communication, but the Bible does not limit Jesus's communication to mere words. Jesus not only preached a message—he was and is the message. John's Gospel makes this abundantly clear, declaring at the beginning that Jesus is "The true light, which enlightens everyone … coming into the world" (John 1:9). When Jesus preached, the message was really all about him. He himself was the content of all his sermons—he was and is the Savior. He proclaimed himself to be "the light of the world"

(John 8:12), and in so doing, the communicator became the communication of his own sermon.

Jesus's disciples were also Spirit-illumined communicators. Jesus comforted them by reassuring them that they would not be left without help. He promised that when he left they would receive the same empowerment to communicate that he had. He said, "But the Helper, the Holy Spirit, whom the Father will send in my name, he will teach you all things and bring to your remembrance all that I have said to you" (John 14:26).

It is significant that the Holy Spirit's operation is connected to truth—here specifically with *teaching* and *remembering* truth. It is no accident that the apostle John referred to the Holy Spirit as "the Spirit of truth" (see, for example, John 15:26; 16:13), confirming the natural link between the Spirit's ministry and revelation. The Spirit is invisible and he moves where he will (see John 3:8), but this does not mean that the ministry of the Spirit should be understood subjectively as mere feelings or intuition; rather, it is marked by and connected to the Word that he inspired (2 Tim. 3:16). Do not dare to confuse the work of the Spirit with mere human emotions—that is, following emotions as the guide for spiritual life. This is a dangerous trend in the church that takes people off in so many different directions. The Spirit has not left believers to this kind of subjectivity but instead uses the Word of God to provide objective wisdom for all of life's decisions (Josh. 1:8–10; Ps. 119:105; 2 Peter 1:3).

This link between the Spirit's ministry and revelation is repeated in the book of Acts in accounts of Spirit-empowered preaching. Time and time again the Spirit of God illumined leaders of the early church to communicate truth and to effect change. Peter's sermon at Pentecost, when he quoted from the Old Testament Minor Prophet Joel, documented the historic beginning of the New Testament church and showed that what Joel had prophesied was partially being fulfilled. This is what theologians call the "Already/Not Yet" principle.[27] At Pentecost Peter understood that the Holy Spirit was being poured out in a new and significant way on the early church disciples, and he interpreted what was happening according to Old Testament prophecy:

"And in the last days it shall be," God declares, "that I will pour out my Spirit on all flesh, and your sons and your daughters shall prophesy,
and your young men shall see visions,
and your old men shall dream dreams;
even on my male servants and female servants
in those days I will pour out my Spirit, and they shall prophesy ..."   (Acts 2:17–18)

Peter was given the spiritual discernment to make this connection, and he brought a Spirit-empowered message, which in turn brought about massive transformation. Acts 2 recounts this spiritual yield of 3,000 souls who received the Word, were baptized, and were added to the church (Acts 2:41).

Stephen, an early church preacher, was identified as a man "full of grace and power" (Acts 6:8–10). When Stephen went to preach in an eclectic synagogue, the leaders there rose to dispute with him but "they could not withstand the wisdom and the Spirit with which he was speaking" (Acts 6:10). Luke says of Stephen that he was filled with "wisdom." It could be said this way: He taught as one filled with the Holy Spirit. He was illumined to speak. The Spirit of God was with Stephen to such an extent that the countenance of this church evangelist shone "like the face of an angel" (Acts 6:15).

Stephen went to preach before Israel's high priest and council, and Acts 7 is the record of his mighty sermon, a sermon he preached with his life on the line. His approach was a simple delivery, and he preached the straight story of redemptive history. He began with the call of Abraham and from there unfolded the early biblical record all the way to the coming of Jesus, "the Righteous One" (Acts 7:52). The more he communicated God's character, the more convicted and enraged his hearers became. Ultimately, their rage-filled hard-hearted response turned this tribunal into a murder scene. Stephen, illumined by the Spirit, responded to their decision to kill him with an incredibly godly focus. Acts records, "But he, full of the Holy Spirit, gazed into heaven and saw the glory of God, and Jesus standing at the right hand of God. And he said, 'Behold, I see the heavens opened, and the Son of Man standing at the right hand of God'" (Acts 7:55–56).

From an account like this it is clear that the Spirit illumines a man's mind as he is ministering the truth. As we noted earlier, the apostle Paul was a man who did not trust in his preaching style or methods, but rather relied on the simple illumined truth of the Word. The basis of his communication was that he was illumined to believe in truth. Because of this, Paul's preaching method was simple and an example to be followed. Paul summarized this in 2 Corinthians 4:13, where he wrote, "I believed, and so I spoke." Why did Paul preach? The Spirit of God had given him faith, and communication followed. It really is that simple.

The remarkable account in Acts 9 of Paul's conversion illustrates this well. Paul was on his way to Damascus, "breathing threats and murder against the disciples of the Lord" and ready to find all the followers of Jesus to tie them up and haul them back to Jerusalem (Acts 9:1–2). The Lord intervened: "… suddenly a light from heaven flashed around him" (Acts 9:3). The Lord Jesus knocked Paul to the ground and confronted him, asking, "… why are you persecuting me?" (Acts 9:4). In this account, the light was the presence of the Lord (1 Tim. 6:16) and it was used to blind Paul for three days. Paul's physical blindness was indicative of his spiritual blindness, because at the end of three days Paul's conversion was evidenced by two things. First, "something like scales fell from his eyes," and second, "he rose and was baptized" (Acts 9:18). Not only could Paul now see physically, but he could also now see spiritually. So what was Paul's immediate response? He ate some food and "… immediately he proclaimed Jesus in the synagogues, saying, 'He is the Son of God'" (Acts 9:19–20). He was illumined, and he preached; "I believed, and so I spoke."

What do these passages from Acts 9 have in common? That the preacher is illumined by the truth to speak the truth. His communication is based on illumination. As the passages above reveal, this is the work the Holy Spirit does for the preacher as the preacher interacts with the truth. The one who desires to preach truth must long for the Spirit to illumine his mind. Those who communicate for God must be as passionate as King David was to retain an illumined preaching ministry, literally begging for God's anointing from the Holy Spirit (Ps. 51:11).

Richard Averbeck, a theological scholar, recognizes how much of biblical teaching today, especially in institutions and seminaries, is dry, perfunctory, and mechanical when the truth does not first inflame the teacher or professor. He believes that biblical scholars and preachers alike need to study, not just to get the biblical message right, but also to be illumined and affected by what is being learned. Averbeck delivers the challenge that "what we need to engage in is the kind of biblical scholarship in which the Bible is not only the subject of investigation, but the investigation itself *turns back upon the scholar in a transforming way* ... [and] this is what illumination is all about" (emphasis added).[28] Averbeck calls scholars to "welcome the Holy Spirit," that the Spirit may

... do what he intends to do through his word in our study, our lives, and our ministries. This work of the Holy Spirit is sometimes called "illumination," the goal of which is to bring the word of God to bear so "that the eyes of" our "hearts" may be "enlightened" (Eph. 1:18; note "the Spirit of wisdom and revelation" in v. 17 [NIV]).[29]

In other words, the illumined preacher or teacher is called to pass on the very truths about which he was first illumined through personal study. Averbeck speaks insightfully about the fact that "Scholarly study of the Bible can be done either in a way that invites the Holy Spirit to do his transforming work through his word, or in a way that suffocates the work of the Spirit in the scholar's study, and in his or her life and ministry."[30]

Whether Old Testament scholars like Averbeck or preachers, those studying the Word of God must study not just to get the biblical message right, but also to be impacted and illumined by what is personally learned. Many preachers think that the Spirit's work of illumination is the rare exception and seem to believe that the Spirit sometimes mystically gives extra insights into the text of Scripture. Not so! The case made by the passages we have examined is that the preacher should expect the ministry of illumination to be a necessary component in his own study and in the act of preaching. Again, the "Bible is ... the subject of investigation...[which] *turns back upon the scholar in a transforming way.*"[31]

Having this in mind, the Bible student and communicator should maintain that the goal of the study is to have a "transformed life of love from a pure [heart], a good conscience and a sincere faith."[32] He should also approach the study to have an "encounter with God ... in submission to the Word."[33] This must culminate with the preacher or teacher "guiding others to read their own Bibles to be affected in the same way the communicator was."[34] The preacher must always have the goal of personal transformation in his mind as he studies the text. When God's Word and his Spirit transform the preacher's heart and actions through study, prayer, and meditation, then and only then can the preacher authentically model the transforming work of illumination to his hearers as the Word is preached. This kind of authenticity does not guarantee that the hearers will be affected, illumined, or transformed (see Chapter 3 on condemnation), but the preacher's conscience can be clear, however the Lord chooses to work. Preaching in this way is truly first and foremost a ministry of worship as an offering to God (see Rom. 15:16).

To be an authentic communicator, what is required is diligent study in God's Word and submissiveness to the work of the Spirit in life and ministry. Only then should the preacher expect his preaching to be what John Owen called the "instrumental cause" of conversions and convictions.[35] Preaching is God's biblical method, but to do it right the preacher must seek authentic illumination.

Illumination by means of communication

If we now return to the passage in 2 Corinthians 4 that is central to this discussion of illumination, we see not only how crucial it is for God to first illumine communicators to preach, but also what the Scriptures attest as the specific method by which the Lord illumines people. What is the actual process whereby God opens blind eyes to see? Paul said in 2 Corinthians 4:5, "… what we *proclaim* is not ourselves, but Jesus Christ as Lord, with ourselves as your servants for Jesus' sake." Paul wanted people to make no mistake about this matter. He wanted his ministry to be viewed in terms of his own self-deprecation. He made it crystal clear that the reason why people believed and saw the glory of Christ was not because Paul promoted himself or his leadership abilities, but rather because he promoted the gospel. Paul claims that he did just one thing—he preached "Jesus Christ as Lord." In this way, Paul depicted himself merely as the instrument or tool through which the life-changing message flowed. The change-agent is always the gospel—the message the apostle Peter called the "imperishable" seed (1 Peter 1:23). Paul made this same point in

2 Corinthians 3, saying that the only hope for unbelieving Jews who were "hardened" and unable to make the connection from the old covenant law to Christ was to have their blindness lifted "through Christ" (2 Cor. 3:14).

Here is the point: It is only the gospel message that Jesus is Lord that rips away the veil, allowing a person to "turn to the Lord" (2 Cor. 3:16). Paul knew that there is no human way to change people's hearts—only God's Word can do this work. At the same time, Paul recognized that he was a "jar of clay"—a common household nondescript clay pot that God designed to contain "treasure" (2 Cor. 4:7). Even though Paul, as a clay pot, knew he could never take credit for the heart change that occurred when people came to Christ, he was not passive—he preached (2 Cor. 4:5, 13).

Though it is the Word of God that changes people's hearts, the Bible repeatedly asserts that preaching is the dominant functional way by which God communicates truth, enlightening souls trapped in darkness. As we have seen, Paul's testimony attests that as soon as he was illumined he "immediately ... proclaimed Jesus in the synagogues, saying, 'He is the Son of God'" (Acts 9:20). Preaching was this man's life calling. It was as if this was all he could possibly do. Christ had revealed himself to Paul, bringing the light of the gospel to his soul, and so Paul gave his entire being to proclaiming this same revelation in order to bring that light to his kinsmen as well as to the Gentiles. Paul spoke of this when he stood before King Agrippa, telling how he had seen "a light from heaven, brighter than the sun" (Acts 26:13). Jesus had revealed himself to Paul, giving Paul his marching orders, saying,

> I have appeared to you for this purpose, to appoint you as a servant and witness to the things in which you have seen me and to those in which I will appear to you, delivering you from your people and from the Gentiles—to whom I am sending you *to open their eyes, so that they may turn from darkness to light and from the power of Satan to God,* that they may receive forgiveness of sins and a place among those who are sanctified by faith in me. (Acts 26:16–18)

For Paul, his whole life boiled down to the fact that he was a "witness"; he had seen the resurrected Christ and was appointed to be a spokesman, a communicator of what he had both physically and spiritually seen. Note once again: Paul was called to preach because preaching God's Word opens blind eyes!

Paul continued to describe exactly what his preaching ministry looked like, testifying to King Agrippa, "O King Agrippa, I was not disobedient to the heavenly vision, but *declared* first to those in Damascus, then in Jerusalem and throughout all the region of Judea, and also to the Gentiles, that they should repent and turn to God, performing deeds in keeping with their repentance" (Acts 26:19–20).

Paul used a word here that is synonymous with "preached." He said that he "declared," or "announced," with the purpose of "open[ing] their eyes" and "turn[ing] [his hearers] from darkness to light and from the power of Satan to God" (Acts 26:18). Plain and simple, preaching facilitates illumination.

There are two further clear examples of how preaching opened blind eyes. First, there is the example of when Philip preached to the Ethiopian eunuch, who was the high-ranking court official of the queen of the Ethiopians (Acts 8:27). Philip was spiritually led to run up alongside this man's chariot to ask what he was reading. As it turned out, the eunuch was reading about Jesus as the suffering servant from Isaiah 53. What is interesting is the way Philip asked the question. He said, "Do you understand what you are reading?" (Acts 8:30). Philip was not asking in terms of this man's intellect or comprehension, but in terms of his spiritual apprehension. Throughout Scripture, when a person is said to *understand* truth it can most often be equated with spiritual illumination. This, by the way, is instructive for anyone attempting to evangelize lost people. Evangelism can be boiled down to asking spiritual questions and listening to the responses. Philip was testing the eunuch to see if the Holy Spirit had illumined him yet. Reading the account, it appears that within that very exchange the Spirit was indeed opening this man's heart, because he said, "How can I, unless someone guides me?" (Acts 8:31). This showed Philip that the eunuch was open to hear truth, so, as Luke records, "Philip opened his mouth, and beginning with this Scripture he told him the good news about Jesus" (Acts 8:35). Though this was one-on-one communication, Philip opened his mouth and the Spirit opened the eunuch's blind eyes.

A second noteworthy example of the communication of truth illumining a person's heart is in Acts 16:13–14. This is the account of how Paul, Silas, and Timothy "… sat down and spoke" to a group of women outside the gate at Philippi. As they did so, one woman, named Lydia, was converted. Luke recounts that she "heard" the message that was spoken and that "The Lord opened her heart to pay attention to what was said by Paul" (Acts 16:14). On a functional level, Paul spoke the truth, and that was all it took. The Lord took over, opening Lydia's heart "to pay attention to what was said." This is another way of saying she was illumined by preaching to spiritually apprehend the message preached.

Implications for the preacher

At this point, we need to remember how important it is to properly understand the nature of the book that preachers are to communicate. Sometimes when preaching is emphasized it can be easy to forget that the power of preaching is bound up in the message, not the speech-act. Though it is important to understand the biblical case that the Spirit's involvement is a necessity in order for the preacher or hearer to be illumined, it is equally crucial to understand the nature of the book the Spirit originally wrote (2 Tim. 3:16; 2 Peter 1:21). The Bible is a God-inspired book that is meant to communicate. It is not merely what scholars call "locutionary"—it simply "says something"—but it is "illocutionary,"[36] that is, "it *does* something."[37] Though the Bible is objective, it is written with the purpose of warning, asserting, and promising.[38] The Bible is also what scholars call "perlocutionary": It is a book addressing real people in real time.[39] It is a book that, by nature, not only informs but also persuades and "invites a response," making it "interlocutionary."[40]

The Bible itself claims to be inspired by the Holy Spirit (2 Tim. 3:16), alive, and powerful (Heb. 4:12). These attributes separate it from every other piece of written material for all time. How freeing it is for the preacher to come to grips with the fact that the Scripture, not the speaker, is the change-agent! The speaker must, of course, do all he can to narrow the distance between the "ancient author" of the text and the "modern reader,"[41] but he must always do this recognizing that it is the Word that does the work of illumination.

Once again, recognizing the nature of the Scriptures should take pressure off the communicator, because God's Word was written as a book to communicate. The preacher dare not allow himself to cave in to the pressure to overemphasize speaking methodologies from postmodern preachers such as Doug Pagitt or preaching mentors such as Fred Craddock. Any preaching style or method is, in and of itself, superficial and unable to affect real spiritual change in the hearts of people. The Bible calls for men of God to preach with clarity and simplicity—leaving the Spirit to do his work of opening hearts and allowing people to see the glory of Jesus and his gospel. As Paul told Timothy, "preach the word" (2 Tim. 4:2). This Word is God's own living and powerful book, inspired and fashioned to communicate.

Notes

1 **Doug Pagitt,** *Preaching Re-Imagined: The Role of the Sermon in Communities of Faith* (Grand Rapids, MI: Zondervan, 2005), p. 23.

2 Ibid.

3 Ibid. p. 21.

4 Ibid. p. 27.

5 **Mark Shivers,** *"Preaching Re-Imagined:* A Review," at: theOoze.com.

6 **Andy Rowell,** "Review of *Preaching Re-Imagined* by Doug Pagitt," Church Leadership Conversations, February 26, 2006, at: andyrowell.net.

7 **Pagitt,** *Preaching Re-Imagined,* p. 233.

8 **Shivers,** *"Preaching Re-Imagined:* A Review."

9 **Pagitt,** *Preaching Re-Imagined,* p. 126.

10 Ibid. p. 137.

11 **Robert Stephen Reid,** *"Preaching Re-Imagined:* The Role of the Sermon in Communities of Faith," in *The Christian Century,* August 22, 2006, p. 39.

12 **Pagitt,** *Preaching Re-Imagined,* pp. 115–117.

13 Ibid. p. 117.

14 Ibid.

15 **Kent Anderson,** review of **Pagitt,** *Preaching Re-Imagined,* at: preaching.org.

16 **Pagitt,** *Preaching Re-Imagined,* p. 197.

17 Ibid. p. 247.

18 Pagitt does make reference to the Holy Spirit's work, but it is in the context of being willing

to listen to unbelievers on matters of faith and Christianity. **Pagitt,** *Preaching Re-Imagined,* pp. 224–225.

19 Fred B. Craddock, *As One Without Authority* (St. Louis, MI: Chalice Press, 2001).

20 R. Eugene Ownes, review of **Craddock,** *As One Without Authority,* in *Perspectives in Religious Studies,* 7/3 (1980), pp. 246–247.

21 Craddock, *As One Without Authority,* p. 57.

22 Kent Anderson, review of **Craddock,** *As One Without Authority,* at: preaching.org.

23 Craddock, *As One Without Authority,* pp. 80–81.

24 Stephen Farris, review of **Craddock,** *As One Without Authority,* in *Homiletic,* 27/1 (2002), pp. 35–36.

25 Fred B. Craddock, "Preaching: An Appeal to Memory," in **Mike Graves,** (ed.), *What's the Matter with Preaching Today?* (Louisville, KY: Westminster John Knox Press, 2004), p. 60.

26 Ibid. p. 66.

27 Herman Ridderbos, trans. **John Richard de Witt,** *Paul: An Outline of his Theology* (1966; 1975, Grand Rapids, MI: Eerdmans), pp. 251, 306.

28 Richard E. Averbeck, "God, People, and the Bible: The Relationship between Illumination and Biblical Scholarship," in **Daniel B. Wallace** and **M. James Sawyer,** (eds.), *Who's Afraid of the Holy Spirit? An Investigation into the Ministry of the Spirit of God Today* (Dallas: Biblical Studies Press, 2005), p. 137.

29 Ibid. p. 139.

30 Ibid.

31 Ibid. p. 137.

32 (1 Tim. 1:5), ibid.

33 Ibid.

34 Ibid.

35 John Owen, *The Holy Spirit: His Gifts and Power* (Grand Rapids, MI: Kregel, 1954), p. 137.

36 Kevin J. Vanhoozer, *Is There a Meaning in This Text? The Bible, the Reader, and the Morality of Literary Knowledge* (Grand Rapids, MI: Zondervan, 1998), pp. 32–33.

37 Averbeck, "God, People, and the Bible," p. 144. Averbeck summarizes Vanhoozer's treatment of speech-act theory as it relates to the ministry of the Holy Spirit and preaching, from **Vanhoozer's** *Is There a Meaning in This Text?* and "Introduction: Hermeneutics, Text, and Biblical Theology," in *New International Dictionary of Old Testament Theology and Exegesis* (Grand Rapids, MI: Zondervan, 1999).

38 Vanhoozer, *Is There a Meaning?,* pp. 410–413.

39 Ibid.

40 Ibid.

41 Averbeck, "God, People, and the Bible," pp. 139–140.

Conversion by illumination

What are the glorious consequences of faithfully communicating the gospel? Seeing people come to Christ! This is one of the highest joys for any believer, and it is an exciting and unforgettable experience to be used by the Lord as a change-agent to bring people into the Kingdom. Can you remember times when you were used by God to be his mouthpiece to speak words of eternal life to others? It is humbling and inspiring at the same time. It is so easy to fail to make this mission of the gospel a priority, yet giving the gospel—"the ministry of reconciliation" (2 Cor. 5:18)—is one of the primary reasons why Christians are here on earth.

It is clear from 2 Corinthians 4 that it is the Word that ignites illumination in a person's heart and that believers are often instrumental in this process as they speak the truth. Conversion is the miracle whereby God creates light in a person's soul. Paul testified of his own conversion experience, saying, "For God, who said, 'Let light shine out of darkness,' has shone in our hearts" (2 Cor. 4:6). This describes the Lord's illuminating work in Paul's own heart when he was converted. So what actually happens when a person is converted—when the lights come on?

Old Testament passages

There are two important passages in the Old Testament that vividly picture what it looks like when a person is converted. The first passage is the prophet Jeremiah's prophecy of the new covenant, which he describes by saying, "But this is the covenant that I will make with the house of Israel after those days, declares the LORD: I will put my law within them, and I will write it on their hearts. And I will be their God, and they shall be my people" (Jer. 31:33).

Jeremiah was, at this point in Judah's history, speaking of Israel's and Judah's need for heart transformation. God's nation had failed under the Mosaic covenant, and so God spoke through his prophet to provide the answer to the nation's dilemma, bringing a new covenant of heart change. This was a covenant with Israel and only took effect with the remnant who were granted conversion (Rom. 11:5); however, the new covenant was also applied to the church. Though Jeremiah was not aware of this application of his prophecy, the new covenant is the banner for all conversion that takes place in the New Testament church (2 Cor. 3:6).

Ezekiel is the second prophet who prophesied of this same thing: "And I will give you a new heart, and a new spirit I will put within you. And I will remove the heart of stone from your flesh and give you a heart of flesh. And I will put my Spirit within you, and cause you to walk in my statutes and be careful to obey my rules" (Ezek. 36:26–27). Like Jeremiah, Ezekiel was speaking of spiritual heart transformation for the nation of Israel. His prophecy was pointing to new-covenant heart transformation that is now experienced in the church, whereby "the Spirit gives life" (2 Cor. 3:6).

New Testament passages
In the Gospels, New Testament conversion begins with Jesus. He is repeatedly seen offering the Kingdom, discerning who was truly part of it and who was not. Jesus's disciples were not exempt from being put to this same test. Remember that Jesus questioned the Twelve as to whether they truly knew whom they were following. Jesus asked, "But who do you say that I am?" and Peter, no doubt first to respond, said, "You are the Christ, the Son of the living God" (Matt. 16:15–16). What is interesting is what Jesus discerned from Peter's answer. Jesus said, "Blessed are you, Simon Bar-Jonah! For flesh and blood has not revealed this to you, but my Father who is in heaven" (Matt. 16:17). When Jesus declared Peter to be "blessed," he was affirming not only that the Holy Spirit had provided him with the correct answer, but also that Peter had truly been converted. He had a "blessed" spiritual status. Peter was not just another curious follower, still waiting to be convinced that Jesus was Messiah. His heart had been transformed by illumined revelation.

There were many people following Jesus, watching him preach and perform miracles, whom Jesus discerned were not part of the Kingdom. According to John's Gospel, the Lord was careful not to entrust himself to those who did not truly believe (John 2:24). He knew that genuine conversion was more than an adjustment of a person's will or disposition whereby a person would merely acknowledge Jesus as a powerful speaker or miracle worker. Jesus's ministry always defined conversion as that which comes only by the Spirit of God and which totally transforms a person's heart.

Perhaps the clearest example of this is in John 3, where the Lord met the Pharisee named Nicodemus. Nicodemus set up this meeting with Jesus during the night, perhaps out of fear for his own reputation as a religious leader. He would not want to be seen with Jesus, who was known as a radical. Though Nicodemus affirmed Jesus as a respected rabbi or teacher with a unique connection with God, Jesus discerned that this was a superficial response. Jesus approached him with a test, saying, "Truly, truly, I say to you, unless one is born again he cannot see the kingdom of God" (John 3:3). Jesus further clarified this, saying, "That which is born of the flesh is flesh, and that which is born of the Spirit is spirit. Do not marvel that I said to you, 'You must be born again'" (John 3:6–7). By these statements Jesus showed that being converted by the Spirit of God is as dramatic as being physically born in the first place. He then made it clear that only when a person experiences spiritual conversion does he or she "see the kingdom of God" (John 3:3). Jesus was emphatic with Nicodemus about the Spirit's essential role in conversion.

Again, in John 6, knowing that the crowds were seeking his miracles more than they were seeking him, Jesus said, "It is the Spirit who gives life; the flesh is no help at all. The words that I have spoken to you are spirit and life" (John 6:63). Jesus was clear that no amount of human effort will give anybody spiritual life since "the flesh is no help at all." However, when the Holy Spirit opens a person's heart, the words of Jesus become "spirit and life." It is the Spirit of God energizing the Word that converts those who are blind, causing them to see.

Statements from church history

Martin Luther, the father of the Reformation, wrote of the link between the power of the Holy Spirit and the Word of God. According to Luther's perspective, "the written Word of the Scriptures is always indissolubly joined with the power of the Holy Spirit ... [who] operates on and in the hearts and minds of those who properly hear and read it."[1] Calvin, along the same lines, said that the "Scripture will ultimately suffice for a saving knowledge of God only when its certainty is founded upon the inward persuasion of the Holy Spirit."[2]

In the same theological vein, Jonathan Edwards understood that illumined knowledge is the crucial "… key that first opens the hard heart, and enlarges the affections, and so opens the way for men into the kingdom of heaven" (see Luke 11:52).[3] Perhaps B. B. Warfield best summarized how the Word and Spirit work together when he wrote of how the objective revelation "embodied in the Scriptures" and the subjective operation of the Spirit enable a person who is darkened by sin to receive revelation. He said that "by … [a] conjoint divine action, objective and subjective, a true knowledge of God is communicated to the human soul."[4] As the Word and Spirit work together, "… the testimony of the Spirit is the subjective preparation of the heart to receive the objective evidence in a sympathetic embrace."[5]

So, throughout church history, men of God have consistently affirmed that conversion comes by the Spirit illuminating the Word of God. At precisely the point of conversion, when the soul is regenerated by the Spirit, there is created in the soul a heartfelt embrace of the truth. This is when the Spirit initially impresses the Scripture on the heart, conscience, will, and affections of a person. Once this action is initiated, it continues throughout the believer's spiritual life.

The example of Paul

The radical conversion of the apostle Paul is a striking example of spiritual conversion. He was a man transformed by the Holy Spirit and by the revelation of Jesus. Prior to conversion, Paul was known for being "a persecutor of the church" (Phil. 3:6) and "a blasphemer, persecutor, and insolent opponent" (1 Tim. 1:13). To top it all off, he called himself "the foremost" of sinners (1 Tim. 1:15). His conversion was unique and obviously different in at least two ways from the conversion a person experiences today: His conversion included the calling to be an apostle, and this required him to be an eyewitness of the resurrected Christ (Acts 26:16; 1 Cor. 9:1). Even so, there is overlap with what all believers experience, specifically regarding illumination. All who are saved are illumined. Note again Paul's testimony in Acts 9, but this time in terms of his conversion. Luke wrote,

Now as he went on his way, he approached Damascus, and suddenly a light from heaven flashed around him. And falling to the ground he heard a voice saying to him, "Saul, Saul, why are you persecuting me?" And he said, "Who are you, Lord?" And he said, "I am Jesus, whom you are persecuting." (Acts 9:3–5)

There is some debate as to whether Paul's conversion took place when the Lord confronted him in verses 3–5 or later when Ananias met him in Damascus. The strongest evidence that Paul's conversion happened on the road to Damascus is that the Lord there commissioned him to be an apostle to the Gentiles. Paul's testimony confirms this. Paul quoted Jesus as having said,

I have appeared to you for this purpose, to appoint you as a servant and witness to the things in which you have seen me and to those in which I will appear to you, delivering you from your people and from the Gentiles—to whom I am sending you to open their eyes, so that they may turn from darkness to light and from the power of Satan to God, that they may receive forgiveness of sins and a place among those who are sanctified by faith in me. (Acts 26:16–18)

The scriptural support for the position that Paul's conversion occurred later is found in the context of Acts 9 when he met with Ananias. It is recorded that "something like scales fell from his eyes" (Acts 9:18), which could symbolize either the illuminating work of the Spirit that had already taken place on the road to Damascus or the work that was taking place at that moment with Ananias in Damascus.

From Acts 9 we can identify three features that Paul's conversion has in common with the conversions of all believers everywhere. First of all, spiritual conversion involves dramatic transformation. This is impossible to miss from the account of Paul's conversion. Of course, knowing Paul's pre-conversion state highlights this, and in some ways causes his conversion to stand out as a more remarkable example than most. Remember who Paul was? Paul was transformed from chief persecutor of

Christians to chief apostle. He stood out among the Pharisees for the fervor with which he captured and sanctioned death sentences for all those "belonging to the Way" (Acts 9:2). Paul, himself later persecuted for his faith, testified of his own participation in the martyrdom of the evangelist Stephen. He was not merely present when Stephen's blood was shed, but was functioning as supervisor, "... standing by and approving and watching over the garments of those who killed him" (Acts 22:20). The Jerusalem church knew his reputation well, having heard so much about this zealous young Pharisee. They knew so much about him that they did not immediately trust him. When Paul turned up to "join the disciples ... they were all afraid of him, for they did not believe that he was a disciple" (Acts 9:26).

As extraordinary a conversion as this was, the Bible teaches that all true conversions, from a spiritual standpoint, are extraordinary. Even though from the human (and therefore surface) perspective Paul's testimony and conversion experience appear more dramatic than those of the average believer, all conversions are acts of God. In all conversions people are "... delivered ... from the domain of darkness and transferred ... to the kingdom of his beloved Son" (Col. 1:13). No matter how it looks from the human vantage point, each conversion is amazing. Paul is emphatic in Romans 1:16 that the "gospel" is the "power of God for salvation to everyone who believes." All newly converted people have had "the righteousness of God ... *revealed*" to them by faith (Rom. 1:17), which again comes back to the work of the Holy Spirit, who opens blind eyes to grasp the truth and glory of the gospel.

A second commonality between Paul's conversion and all conversions is the revelation of truth by the Holy Spirit. Note how Paul testified of this when he wrote to the churches of Galatia: "For I would have you know, brothers, that the gospel that was preached by me is not man's gospel. For I did not receive it from any man, nor was I taught it, but I received it through a revelation of Jesus Christ" (Gal. 1:11–12). Paul placed his preaching ministry in the background to emphasize that the power to transform souls came solely from the gospel message itself. What he preached was "not man's gospel"—not something contrived by a mere man—but instead "received ... through a revelation of Jesus Christ." Paul received direct revelation from Christ, but all believers are illumined by the Holy Spirit as to the truth of Jesus Christ; all have Jesus revealed to them.

A third commonality of all conversions is this: When Paul spoke of receiving revelation, he was not referring to seeing Christ with his eyes (even though he did in fact see him) but to hearing him with his ears. Remember from Acts 9:3–5 that Paul was blinded by the glorious flash of light around him and that "… falling to the ground he *heard* a voice" which said, "I am Jesus" (Acts. 9:3–5). Paul's conversion came from *hearing* the truth of the gospel. He said the same thing to the Romans when he wrote to them that people *see* spiritually by *hearing* the truth: "… faith comes from hearing, and hearing through the word of Christ" (Rom. 10:17). When a person's eyes are opened to embrace Jesus, he or she does not need one shred of extra-biblical or historical evidence to seal the deal. There is no need for evidential apologetics. Whether or not the new believer understands it at that point in time, the gospel truth is what has saved him or her, not a personal cerebral convincing of the truth. The gospel is always what reveals Jesus. John Piper said it this way:

Jesus, as he is revealed in the Bible, has a glory—an excellence, a spiritual beauty—that can be seen as self-evidently true. It is like seeing the sun and knowing that it is light and not dark, or like tasting honey and knowing that it is sweet and not sour … How can they know him and be sure of him? What they "see" is the *verbal portrayal* of Jesus in the Gospel, that is, in the apostolic preaching of Christ.[6]

Conversion comes through hearing words of truth, hearing this "verbal portrayal of Jesus." Whether a person reads the Word and hears it in his or her mind, or actually hears words spoken aloud to his or her physical ears, this is the way it happens for anybody who has ever been converted.[7]

Back in 2 Corinthians 4, conversion is described as an act of the Creator. Simply put, God creates light in people's hearts. Remember that Paul drew a direct parallel between God as the creator of physical light—"For God, who said, 'Let light shine out of darkness'"—and God as the creator of spiritual light—"has shone in our hearts to give the light of the knowledge of the glory of God in the face of Jesus Christ" (2 Cor. 4:6). This is the picture of what happens in the heart when someone is converted. A person held captive in spiritual darkness by sin and Satan is suddenly enlightened to see God's glory "in the face of Jesus."

This is a work in which God "awakens [people], as from the dead, to see and taste the divine reality of God in Scripture, which authenticates itself as God's own word."[8] Conversion is "the immediate, unassailable, life-giving revelation to the mind of the majesty of God manifest in the Scriptures themselves."[9] Under this banner, "*Illumination* ... in principle [is] that gift granted to the child of God, from the very moment of his new birth, which permits him to see the kingdom of God (John 3:3) ... [and which is] normally permanent and increasing."[10] Jonathan Edwards summarized a believer's new perspective thus: "Things that appertain to the way of salvation by Christ are opened to him in a new manner, and he now understands those divine and spiritual doctrines which once were foolishness to him."[11]

The Word of God makes it unmistakably clear that a person's conversion is entirely the work of God. Piper put it this way:

... God witnesses to us of his reality and the reality of his Son and his Word by giving us life from the dead so that we come alive to his majesty and *see* him for who he is in his Word. In that instant we do not reason from premises to conclusions, we see that we are awake, and there is not even a prior human judgment about it to lean on. When Lazarus wakened in the tomb by the call or the "witness" of Christ, he knew without reasoning that he was alive and that this call wakened him [emphasis added].[12]

Implications for the preacher

What impact does understanding the doctrine of illumination in conversion have upon the preacher? The power of conversion is the power of the Holy Spirit bringing light to a blind soul through the Word of God. The power of conversion is the Holy Spirit raising a soul from spiritual death (Eph. 2:5), bringing someone to life spiritually. God invades a soul enthralled by sin and darkness and sets it free, bringing the light of faith (Rom. 1:17). It is wholly of God, wholly by the Spirit's ministry of illumination.

Just as the Word of God faithfully preached brings condemnation to some, so it brings life to others. The Spirit works in concert with the Word and brings illumination to some so that they are able to *hear*, with spiritual ears opened, and *understand*, with hearts enlightened by faith.

Preach the Word, knowing that the Spirit will work. Preach the Word— God will harden some hearts and illumine others. Preach the Word and know, as did the faithful preachers throughout the Bible, that the Lord will give life, will open hearts, and will transfer people from the kingdom of darkness to the "kingdom of his beloved Son" (Col. 1:13).

Notes

1 **J. Theodore Mueller,** "The Holy Spirit and the Scriptures," in **Carl F. H. Henry,** (ed.), *Revelation and the Bible: Contemporary Evangelical Thought* (Grand Rapids, MI: Baker, 1958), p. 276.

2 **John Calvin, John T. McNeill,** (ed.), and **Ford Lewis Battles,** (tr.), *Calvin: Institutes of the Christian Religion*, vols. XX and XXI of **John Baillie, John T. McNeill,** and **Henry P. Van Dusen,** (eds.), *The Library of Christian Classics* (Louisville, KY: Westminster John Knox Press, 1960), p. 80.

3 **Jonathan Edwards,** *The Religious Affections* (1746; 1986, Carlisle, PA: Banner of Truth), p. 192.

4 **B. B. Warfield,** *Calvin and Augustine* (1956; 1980, Philadelphia: Presbyterian and Reformed, 1980), p. 77, n.

5 Ibid. p. 86.

6 **John Piper,** *Seeing and Savoring Jesus Christ* (Wheaton, IL: Crossway, 2004), pp. 119–120.

7 Ibid. p. 120.

8 **John Piper,** "The Divine Majesty of the Word: John Calvin, The Man and His Preaching," Bethlehem Conference for Pastors, February 4, 1997.

9 Ibid.

10 **René Pache, Helen I. Needham,** (tr.), *The Inspiration and Authority of Scripture* (1969; 1992, Salem, WI: Sheffield Publishing), p. 199.

11 **Edwards,** *The Religious Affections*, p. 193.

12 **Piper,** "The Divine Majesty of the Word."

Convictions through illumination

In 1 Corinthians 2:14 Paul wrote, "The natural person does not accept the things of the Spirit of God, for they are folly to him, and he is not able to understand them because they are spiritually discerned." There is some debate as to what Paul meant when he said that "the things of the Spirit" are "folly" or "foolishness." Some believe he was saying that unbelievers, since they do not have the Holy Spirit, have no capacity to cognitively understand the fundamental meaning of Scripture. The Bible is therefore "folly" because it doesn't make sense to unspiritual people. Others state that what Paul meant was that unbelievers, devoid of the Holy Spirit, are unable to gain spiritual convictions about the truthfulness, authority, and significance of Scripture, and see biblical truth as "folly."[1]

Martin Luther supported the second perspective. He believed that there is what he called an "outer and an inner clarity of Scripture."[2] The outer, or external, clarity means that "by the usual laws or rules of language a Christian could understand the Scripture as a written document."[3] However, "Due to man's sinfulness he needs an inward assist so that he might grasp the spiritual Word of God as the Word of God. The Word of God is a spiritual entity and can only be understood *in faith* with the help of the Holy Spirit."[4] This is what he called the "inner clarity of Scripture," and for Luther, the Holy Spirit in this role "was the Hermes from heaven."[5]

John Calvin called this phenomenon of illumination "imprinting." In the answer to question 302 of his *Geneva Catechism*, he said that this spiritual work happens when we receive the text of Scripture "… with the full consent of our conscience, as truth comes down from heaven, submitting ourselves to it in right obedience, loving it with true affection by having it *imprinted* in our hearts, [so that] we may follow it entirely and conform ourselves to it" (emphasis added).[6] This is where the Word obtains "… acceptance in men's hearts, before it is sealed by the inward testimony of the Spirit."[7] In this way a believer affirms the Word "… with utter certainty (just as if we were gazing upon the majesty of God himself) that it [the Word] has flowed to us from the very mouth of God by the ministry of men."[8]

The work of the Spirit Calvin describes as "imprinting" is sometimes referred to by scholars as "impressing." Note how the modern scholar Kevin Vanhoozer used this terminology:

The Spirit illumines the letter by *impressing* its illocutionary force on the reader. Thanks to the illumination of the Spirit, we see and hear speech acts for what they are—warnings, promises, commands, assertions—together with their implicit claim in our minds and hearts. In so doing, the Spirit does not alter but ministers the meaning: "The spiritual sense is the literal sense correctly understood." The distinction between "letter" and "spirit" is precisely that between reading words and grasping what one reads. Likewise, the difference between a "natural" and an "illuminated" understanding is that between holding an opinion and having a deep sense of its profundity."[9]

Likewise note Greg Heisler's definition: "Illumination is the process whereby the Holy Spirit so *impresses*, convinces, and convicts the believer as to the truthfulness and significance of the author's intended meaning in the text that a change in action, attitude, or belief occurs, resulting in a more transformed, Spirit-filled life" (emphasis added).[10]

How does the Bible depict the gaining of spiritual convictions? First comes conversion, in which a person is initially illumined by the Spirit and revelation. At justification, having been illumined, such a person has gained a crucial part of progressive sanctification: spiritual convictions. This is bound up in a simple phrase found back in 2 Corinthians 4.

There Paul described a person's initial illumination, saying that light "... has shone in our hearts to give *the light of the knowledge* of the glory of God in the face of Jesus Christ" (2 Cor. 4:6). When a person is converted or initially illumined, he or she gains what Paul simply called "knowledge." It is clear that, by using this term, he was not talking about academic data. Charles Hodge wrote of this knowledge,

The other truth here taught is, that this knowledge of God in Christ is not a mere matter of intellectual apprehension, which one man may communicate to another. It is a spiritual discernment, to be derived only from the Spirit of God. God must shine into our hearts to give us this knowledge. Matt. 16:17; Gal. 1:16; 1 Cor. 2:10, 14. As the glory of God is spiritual, it must be spiritually discerned. It is therefore easy to see why the Scriptures make true religion to consist in the knowledge of Christ, and why they make the denial of Christ, or want of faith in him as God manifest in the flesh, a soul-destroying sin.[11]

The context of 2 Corinthians 4 speaks of "knowledge" as Spirit-wrought convictions regarding spiritual truth. The Spirit makes the impression on the heart that biblical truth is true. Convincing someone of the absolute certainty of spiritual truth is a work only God can achieve. Paul's Spirit-illumined convictions shaped his entire life—everything he did, spoke, and sacrificed came back to this. He was willing to stake his whole life on what he believed.

Nowhere is this more clearly seen than in what Paul wrote immediately after 2 Corinthians 4:1–6:

We are afflicted in every way, but not crushed; perplexed, but not driven to despair; persecuted, but not forsaken; struck down, but not destroyed; always carrying in the body the death of Jesus, so that the life of Jesus may also be manifested in our bodies. For we who live are always being given over to death for Jesus' sake, so that the life of Jesus also may be manifested in our mortal flesh. So death is at work in us, but life in you. Since we have the same spirit of faith according to what has been written, "I believed, and so I spoke," we also believe, and so we also speak, knowing that he who raised the Lord Jesus will raise us also with Jesus and bring us with you into his presence. (vv. 8–14)

For Paul it was simple. Because he had been illumined to see Jesus he was willing to face horrible persecution and suffering, living as he did under the equivalent of a death sentence. He lived his life as a walking target for Christ-hating persecutors. This text says that he was comforted, knowing that God was using his sacrifice to bring spiritual life to others (2 Cor. 4:12). He lived his life absolutely convinced of this.

In summarizing the power of these spiritual convictions which he possessed, he took a quote from the psalmist to characterize his entire preaching ministry. Paul said, "Since we have the same spirit of faith according to what has been written, 'I believed, and so I spoke,' we also believe, and so we also speak" (2 Cor. 4:13, quoting Ps. 116:10). Paul was simply saying that he lived just like the prophets of old—men who believed truth in a way that drove them to preach no matter the consequences (see Heb. 11:32–38). In other words, the reality of Paul's Spirit-illumined convictions meant he could not contain himself. He was driven to proclaim what *he believed*—his convictions—to anyone who would listen.

Second Corinthians 4:14 tells us exactly what convictions he was referring to, again with the word "knowing" (compare "knowledge" in 2 Cor. 4:6). His conviction was the gospel: "knowing that he who raised the Lord Jesus will raise us also with Jesus and bring us with you into his presence." What made Paul a zealous radical preacher—a madman by the world's standards? He suffered and preached because he was certain that, just as God raised Jesus from the dead, he too would be raised from death with Jesus to be in the Father's presence. This truth, this treasure, was worth giving his life for. Only when a person is illumined, filled with conviction, in this way will he or she follow Jesus in the way in which Jesus calls people to follow him (Matt. 16:24).

Paul knew that he was nothing special. He did not have some extra measure of illumined convictions. This is why he said "*we also* believe, and so *we also* speak" (2 Cor. 4:13) and included all believers, knowing they possessed the same convictions. He gave the same kind of affirmation when he said that he knew the Thessalonians were "chosen" by God because of the way they received the gospel "not only in word, but also in power and in the Holy Spirit and *with full conviction*" (1 Thes. 1:4–4). In his second letter to the Thessalonians, Paul again gave thanks "because God chose" them "to be saved," and here he moved beyond their salvation experience to their sanctification, saying it was "… by the Spirit and belief in the truth" (2 Thes. 2:13). These statements tell how the members of this church were certain, and growing in the certainty, of their beliefs.

Spirit-illumined convictions are always the mark of genuine salvation. Paul's prayer to Timothy was that he would gently correct opponents of the gospel so that "God may perhaps grant them repentance leading to a knowledge of the truth" (2 Tim. 2:25). When a person repents, or turns from sin (see 1 Thes. 1:9), he or she gains and begins to grow in Spirit-illumined convictions, or as Paul said, in "a knowledge of the truth." Paul launched the epistle of Titus by characterizing his entire apostolic ministry as being "for the sake of the faith of God's elect and their knowledge of the truth, which accords with godliness" (Titus 1:1). As with the 2 Timothy passage, the phrase "knowledge of the truth" represents convictions, but here believers gain them at salvation for the purpose of their sanctification or "godliness" (Titus 1:1), as was the case with the Thessalonians. So whether a person is a brand-new believer repenting of sin for the first time, or a decades-old believer still growing in godliness, each possesses spiritually-illumined convictions called the "knowledge of the truth."

Illumined convictions found in a believer's salvation and sanctification are indicative of spiritual appetite. When the psalmist cried out, "Oh, taste and see that the LORD is good!" (Ps. 34:8), this was what he was talking about. In this context, "taste" pictures a person whose soul is filled by the Lord's goodness. Another way to say this is that a person knows—is convinced—that God is good, and he or she is affected or moved by it. The apostle Peter encouraged this kind of spiritual hunger, saying believers should be like "newborn infants" who "long for the pure spiritual milk" in order to grow spiritually (1 Peter 2:2). Peter described what should be the norm for someone who has "tasted that the Lord is good" (1 Peter 2:3) at conversion. It is only natural that, once a person knows that something tastes good, he or she will want more of it. This is how appetite works. A spiritual appetite of this nature is the reason why men of God have, just like the psalmist, begged God, saying, "Open my eyes, that I may behold wondrous things out of your law" (Ps. 119:18). Those with this kind of hunger long for "unveiled discernment, 20/20 spiritual perception" when they read the truth.[12] Their illumined convictions drive them back for more.

Old Testament passages

Some might assume that, since the New Testament says much more about the Holy Spirit than the Old Testament, illumination is primarily a New Testament doctrine. It is easy to forget that Old Testament saints were also illumined by the Spirit of God and had the same kind of spiritual appetites as their New Testament counterparts. The Spirit's involvement in illumining saints may not be as clear in the Old Testament as it is in the New, but from what is known in the New Testament, it is not difficult to infer what was happening for Old Testament believers.

As a first example, let's look in the book of Job, the oldest book of the Bible, to catch a small glimpse of illumination. At the end of the book, the LORD confronts Job after Job has gone through the unbelievable trial of having all of his children struck dead and all his wealth stripped away almost instantaneously. Job was struggling to persevere in faith. One of the ways the Lord exhorted him was by reminding him of who had opened his mind to truth in the first place. The LORD asked him this question: "Who has put wisdom in the inward parts or given understanding to the mind?" (Job 38:36).

Though this example only gives a glimpse at Old Testament illumination, the book of Psalms is much more explicit on the subject. The psalmist says many times that God has opened his mind to grasp spiritual truths. In Psalm 19:7–8, the psalmist extolled the Word of God, saying,

The law of the LORD is perfect,
    reviving the soul;
the testimony of the LORD is sure,
    making wise the simple;
the precepts of the LORD are right,
    rejoicing the heart;
the commandment of the LORD is pure,
    enlightening the eyes.   (Ps. 19:7–8)

Here he declared the convictions that he had regarding the Word of God. He was emphatic that the Word is "perfect," or sound and without error, and that that was what resuscitated his soul. He also spoke of its impeccable testimony and its ability to provide wisdom for the simplest believer. He asserted that the Word is truthful and joy-creating, clean and uncontaminated, and, finally, that it illumines the eyes.

What causes a person to see the Bible in this way? This Old Testament saint did not gain these convictions by scientific, historical, linguistic, or any other academic or interpretive means. This man's eyes were enlightened by the truth itself, by seeing what is so wonderful about this truth. Psalm 119 repeats this same dynamic over and over, saying that the Bible illumines believers to hunger for and love it. These are just a few of the highlights:

- "Make me understand the way of your precepts, and I will meditate on your wondrous works" (v. 27).
- "Your hands have made and fashioned me; give me understanding that I may learn your commandments" (v. 73).
- "Oh how I love your law! It is my meditation all the day. Your commandment makes me wiser than my enemies, for it is ever with me. I have more understanding than all my teachers, for your testimonies are my meditation. I understand more than the aged, for I keep your precepts" (vv. 97–100).
- "How sweet are your words to my taste, sweeter than honey to my mouth! Through your precepts I get understanding; therefore I hate every false way. Your word is a lamp to my feet and a light to my path" (vv. 103–105).
- "The unfolding of your words gives light; it imparts understanding to the simple" (v. 130).
- "Your testimonies are righteous forever; give me understanding that I may live" (v. 144).
- "The sum of your word is truth, and every one of your righteous rules endures forever" (v. 160).
- "Let my cry come before you, O LORD; give me understanding according to your word!" (v. 169).

Much like the psalmist, the prophet Jeremiah had the Word of God revealed to him. These revelations in turn became his convictions. This is pictured by his expression of his appetite, his spiritual hunger for the Word of God, when he said, "Your words were found, and I ate them, and your words became to me a joy and the delight of my heart" (Jer. 15:16).

New Testament passages

JESUS

There is a very clear example in the Gospel of Luke of two late-coming disciples of Christ who were suddenly illumined with convictions. This is the account in Luke 24:13–35 of how Jesus, having just been raised from the dead, met two men on the road to Emmaus. These two were extremely discouraged because, in their minds, their hopes for redemption had been dashed. They believed that their would-be Messiah, Jesus, had failed. The coup that they had hoped would overthrow Rome's rule over their nation was not going to happen. Jesus had been killed (Luke 24:21).

As he often did, Jesus took a very direct approach with these two, calling them "foolish ones … [who were] slow of heart to believe all that the prophets have spoken!" (Luke 24:25). It is amazing to see the way Jesus moved from his rebuke to his revelation. He did not leave these two lost in confusion, but went on to explain himself from the Scriptures: "'Was it not necessary that the Christ should suffer these things and enter into his glory?' And beginning with Moses and all the Prophets, he interpreted to them in all the Scriptures the things concerning himself." Christ Jesus did not appeal to his own authority to reveal himself, he appealed to the written Word of God. Since he was standing right in front of them it would have been so easy for him just to say, "Don't you get it? I'm the one who rose from the dead! I'm Jesus the Messiah!" Instead, however, "he interpreted … the Scriptures … concerning himself" (Luke 24:27). Here the Son of God was seen expositing the Old Testament Scriptures that pointed to his own coming, with the purpose of revealing himself.

By appealing to the Old Testament text, at least the Pentateuch and Prophets, Jesus showed by example what illumines a heart. This is such a grand testimony to the power of the Word of God! As the story goes, the more these disciples heard Jesus's expository teaching, the more they wanted to hear. When Jesus looked as if he might leave, they begged him to stay into the evening. After teaching them for some time, just as they began to eat supper, something amazing happened: These disciples had their "eyes … opened, and they recognized [Jesus]" (Luke 24:31). At this point Jesus vanished, but these men recognized where the illumination came from—the Scriptures. This is clear from their response: "Did not our hearts burn within us while he talked to us on the road, while he opened to us the Scriptures?" (Luke 24:32). Their hearts burned within them, their affections resonated deeply with what Jesus was explaining, "while he opened to us the Scriptures." This is a picture of the Spirit of God making his deep mark on the human heart through the agency of the Word of God as it is explained. Jonathan Edwards, commenting on this narrative, said, "When Christ makes the Scripture a means of the heart's burning with gracious affection, it is by opening the Scriptures to their understanding."[13]

Another example is when Jesus appeared to his eleven apostles and disciples in Jerusalem. It seems reasonable to expect that he would have received a better reception from this group. Unlike the two Jesus met on the road to Emmaus, these were his intimate friends and companions. If anyone could be expected to recognize Jesus and understand what was happening, surely it would be them! Instead, when Jesus appeared to them, rather than them immediately embracing him as the risen Son of God, they were "startled," "frightened," "troubled," had "doubts arise in [their] hearts," and "still disbelieved" (Luke 24:37–41). It was not until they were illumined that they were sure who he was. Luke records that Jesus "… said to them, 'These are my words that I spoke to you while I was still with you, that everything written about me in the Law of Moses and the Prophets and the Psalms must be fulfilled.' Then he opened their minds to understand the Scriptures" (Luke 24:44–45). Once again Jesus used Scripture as the means of opening their minds. Just as before, he appealed to the Old Testament to show that the plan had all along been for the Christ to go to the cross and rise from the dead on the third day (Luke 24:44–47). Once illumined, his disciples were now certain of this.

PAUL

The Spirit's role of illumining believers to have convictions is also a significant theme throughout the epistles. In Romans 8, Paul put the topic of spiritual illumination in the context of mortifying sin. Look at Romans 8:13–16:

For if you live according to the flesh you will die, but if by the Spirit you put to death the deeds of the body, you will live. For all who are led by the Spirit of God are sons of God. For you did not receive the spirit of slavery to fall back into fear, but you have received the Spirit of adoption as sons, by whom we cry, "Abba! Father!" The Spirit himself bears witness with our spirit that we are children of God …

Notice how Paul described illumination. He saw it as taking place when a believer's spirit, or inner man, resonates with the Holy Spirit—when the believer has assurance of his or her salvation, the spiritual conviction that he or she is a child of God. The wonderful point of this text is this: Since Christians are illumined, they are given assurance to obey the Lord, not out of fear, as if they are slaves under an evil master, but instead as adopted children responding to a loving father. Paul says that it is conviction emblazoned upon the heart that motivates believers to kill sin in their lives (Rom. 8:13)!

It is so much easier to walk in sanctification, obeying the Lord, when we are certain of our status as children of God. Christians who do not have this conviction can easily fall into the trap of being moralistic, attempting to be holy by hard work alone. Under the weight of moralism, the Christian experience becomes drudgery. Paul knew this, which is why in Galatians 4:6 he again appealed to our adopted status to combat the nasty sin of legalism.

We have already looked at 1 Corinthians 2:14 in some detail, but it is worthwhile focusing now on one key phrase: Paul affirms that believers have "the mind of Christ" (1 Cor. 2:16). For Paul, being illumined is tantamount to having "the mind of Christ." When Paul says this, he is not espousing some form of mysticism, some kind of ethereal mindset that transcends normal thinking. As demonstrated so far, illumination is always connected to truth and its certainty. In the context of 1 Corinthians 2:12–13 Paul is arguing that there is a contrast between people who think like the world and people who think spiritually. Believers "have received not the spirit of the world, but the Spirit who is from God, that we might understand the things freely given us by God" (1 Cor. 2:12). And what is it that the Spirit helps us to understand? What are "the things freely given us by God?" In verse 13 Paul says that this is the Truth which came through the apostles as "words … taught by the Spirit" (1 Cor. 2:13). This is the inspired Word of God that is imprinted by the Spirit on the soul of the believer. This is what Paul means by believers having the "mind of Christ."

Believers with illumined convictions have spiritual discernment; even though those not illumined might, on a surface level, affirm the Bible, according to Paul they will, deep down, view it as "folly" with no veracity (1 Cor. 2:14).

It is plain to see from these passages that, at its core, the spiritual work of illumination is one whereby the Holy Spirit is impressing truth on the hearts of believers, moving them along from a superficial affirmation of truth to deep personal convictions. Jonathan Edwards described illumination this way when speaking of the believer's affections. He taught that spiritual understanding supercedes what he called "a mere notional understanding," which he compared to knowing "what a triangle is or what a square is." To him, the difference between a man with "a mere notional understanding" and genuine spiritual understanding was the difference between someone "… that has perceived the sweet taste of honey" by actually tasting it and "he who has only looked upon, and felt it."[14] Speaking in reference to 2 Corinthians 2:14, Edwards made this distinction, saying, "There is such a thing … as a spiritual, supernatural understanding of divine things that is peculiar to the saints, and which those who are not saints have nothing of. It is a kind of understanding, apprehending or discerning of divine things, that natural men have nothing of …"[15] For Edwards, this kind of illumined understanding was seeing biblical truth as glorious, having the qualities of supreme beauty and excellence, "the knowledge of the loveliness of divine things."[16]

Perhaps one of the clearest passages on this aspect of illumination providing spiritual convictions is Ephesians 1:17–18. A study of Ephesians shows that one of Paul's chief motives for writing this letter was so that this church could spiritually recognize, see, and comprehend salvation in terms of its present and future implications. A quick perusal of the letter reveals that Paul did not write it in order to right wrongs that were going on at the church in Ephesus. This epistle is not a polemical treatise but is heavenly minded, and was written to encourage the church to grasp the spiritual riches it had received from God.

In Ephesians 1:17–18, Paul stated this banner motivation for everything else he wrote in his epistle: "… that the God of our Lord Jesus Christ, the Father of glory, may give you a spirit of wisdom and of revelation in the knowledge of him, having the eyes of your hearts enlightened, that you may know what is the hope to which he has called you, what are the riches of his glorious inheritance in the saints." Having heard of this church's faith in Jesus and their love for fellow Christians, his affection exploded into his prayer for them (Eph. 1:15). This prayer shows a great deal of his heart, because he prayed this ceaselessly (Eph. 1:16). His prayer was really quite simple. He wanted God to illumine their minds to spiritual realities. He was praying this on the basis of their hearts having already been enlightened (Eph. 1:18). Incidentally, in this context the word "enlightened" would be interchangeable with the term "illuminated" (this is the case in Heb. 10:32 in the New King James Version—the same Greek term is there translated "illuminated").

Paul was desperate for this church to have illumined convictions over spiritual truths. He demonstrated this by using two key phrases: "a spirit of wisdom," and "revelation in the knowledge of him" (Eph. 1:17). To be clear about what Paul was praying for in these phrases, note that these categories are not just temporal gifts that were only for certain believers in the early church. First Corinthians 12:7 says, "*To each* is given the manifestation of the Spirit for the common good," but then verse 8 says, "For *to one* is given through the Spirit ... wisdom, and to another ... knowledge." In verse 7, everyone receives a gift, but in verse 8 there are particular gifts of wisdom and knowledge that not everyone receives. These are for particular believers. What Paul was praying for in Ephesians 1:17, therefore, was that the whole church would receive this blessing of the spirit of wisdom and the knowledge of God—that all believers, with no exceptions, would have this blessing.

Note also that though the "spirit of wisdom" and "revelation" should be taken as categorically separate, they still go hand in hand. They could be viewed as interlocking rings, something like the Olympic rings. Paul wanted the church he loved to possess spiritual "wisdom," which is synonymous with spiritual discernment. It is simply being able to grasp, to comprehend, spiritual realities. He also wanted them to have "revelation," by which he referred to spiritual realities that would not be revealed to a non-spiritually minded person. This word "revelation" implies that a truth or spiritual reality must be unveiled or revealed by the Spirit of God. It is also important to understand that "spirit" here is not referring to the Holy Spirit, but instead to the human spirit or the inner man.[17] In other words, God provides "wisdom and ... revelation" in the believer's inner man or mind.

The immediate context of Ephesians 1 shows that the foundation for Paul's prayer was that the people in this church had been regenerated. In effect, this means that spiritual convictions are like building blocks, built upon the Spirit's initial transforming work that takes place when he saves a person. In his New Testament commentary on Ephesians, John Calvin explained what Paul was saying here. From a grammatical perspective, Calvin understood Paul to be speaking of "a spirit of wisdom and of revelation" by use of metonymy, which restates a concept similarly but not exactly.[18] In this context, Paul used it by first stating that these believers "... were sealed with the promised Holy Spirit" (v. 13), which is the *cause*, then followed this with the *effect*: the believers would gain "a spirit of wisdom and of revelation" (v. 17).

This is also apparent in Paul's phrase "having the eyes of your hearts enlightened" (Eph. 1:18). Instead of this being part of his prayer request for illumination, Paul was affirming what they already had: a spiritual foundation (see Eph. 1:13). The phrase "eyes of your hearts" refers to the mind or inner man. This is a person's seat of affections and thinking, and in this context Paul was writing about that which the Lord spiritually transforms when a person first believes. This word "enlightened," a perfect passive participle, also tells us that this is God turning the lights on, which occurs at salvation. This is the cause or foundation for more illumination. New Testament scholar Homer A. Kent commented in a similar way about this text, saying, "To have such awareness, it was absolutely imperative that ... [the Ephesians] be spiritually enlightened in their hearts ... This had occurred at regeneration ... 'having been enlightened' [which] denotes the present condition resulting from a past act."[19]

In this case, therefore, perhaps a better translation of verses 17–18 would be along the lines of "*since* the eyes of your hearts have been enlightened ... I want you to have spiritual wisdom and revelation." This is what made Paul's request legitimate. He was affirming their capacity to perceive spiritual realities just as a person perceives normal physical life through the five physical senses (see Titus 3:5–6, where the physical image of being washed is used to describe a spiritual reality). As previously noted, Paul mentioned this same reality in 1 Corinthians 2 when he compared the "natural" person with the "spiritual" person (1 Cor. 2:14–15). The spiritual person, someone already regenerate, has built-in discernment to grasp spiritual realities. It is only this person who can grasp "spiritual truths" (1 Cor. 2:13).

What are the spiritual truths that become convictions? Remember that being given a "spirit of wisdom and of revelation" isn't a mystical effect but is grounded in objective truth—"in the knowledge of him" (Eph. 1:17). These spiritual truths are simply knowledge sourced in God himself. It is knowledge that is unique to the sphere of God. When Paul used the word "knowledge," he was speaking of spiritual convictions rather than of academic or cerebral knowledge. It is knowing about what God knows about, or as Paul said elsewhere, it is having "the mind of Christ" (1 Cor. 2:16).

In general, this is simply reading Scripture with an illumined mind. What is refreshing about this is that Paul's prayer was not solely for those with superior thinking abilities, or solely for those in spiritual leadership; all believers have access to illumination. Charles Hodge, commenting on this "knowledge," said, "It is something which all believers need, and for which they should pray."[20] This is for everyone to have, no matter a person's IQ or aptitude.

It always amazes me to see those in the body of Christ without much of an educational background who, by the Spirit's enablement, grasp spiritual truths way beyond those with higher credentials. The psalmist spoke of this idea: "I have more understanding than all my teachers, for your testimonies are my meditation" (Ps. 119:99). No matter where believers find themselves in personal spiritual development, they should pray for and avail themselves of this essential and basic blessing. Pray with the psalmist, "Open my eyes, that I may behold wondrous things out of your law" (Ps. 119:18).

Another reason to see this prayer for the Ephesian believers as important is because Paul prayed the exact same thing for the Colossian believers:

And so, from the day we heard, we have not ceased to pray for you, asking that you may be *filled with the knowledge of his will in all spiritual wisdom and understanding,* so as to walk in a manner worthy of the Lord, fully pleasing to him, bearing fruit in every good work and increasing in the knowledge of God. (Col. 1:9–10)

Whether Paul was praying for the Colossian or Ephesian church, Paul expected these Christians to be able to gain greater levels of spiritual wisdom and revelation. Why? Because of their prior illumination or enlightenment by the Holy Spirit at their salvation (see Eph. 1:18).

What does this greater level of illumination really look like? Again, this is not new revelation but a greater conviction of what has already been revealed to believers. In Ephesians 1, Paul called this "revelation in the knowledge of him" (Eph. 1:17); this is simply knowledge sourced in God. Paul detailed specifically what he meant in the following verses. With laser precision, he pinpointed what he wanted them to know. He said, "… that you may know what is the hope to which he has called you, what are the riches of his glorious inheritance in the saints, and what is the immeasurable greatness of his power toward us who believe, according to the working of his great might …" (Eph. 1:18b–19).

Here he listed three spiritual convictions that they were to gain. See them as three categories: salvation's guarantee, salvation's indescribable wealth, and salvation's inexhaustible power.

First is salvation's *guarantee*. In verse 18 Paul expressed his desire that the Ephesians "… know what is the hope to which he has called [them]." Whenever the word "hope" is used in the context of salvation it is not talking about wishful thinking but a done deal or settled reality. To be "called" essentially means to be summoned by God to salvation by his effectual call. Consequently, this is not simply talking about evangelism, where an appeal is made to someone to believe. This is about God irresistibly drawing a person to saving faith. So here Paul was praying for them to simply come to grips with the reality of a guaranteed place in heaven. For believers to know they are going to heaven produces a deep, settling effect that is essential for being a productive servant of the Lord. Sadly, believers who constantly waver in assurance of salvation often end up wasting time, focusing on themselves instead of on others who are needing encouragement or are needing to hear the gospel.

In the second part of verse 18 Paul moved from the believer's hope of heaven to the possession that is in heaven. He described salvation's *indescribable wealth*, calling it "… the riches of his glorious inheritance in the saints." There are many symbolic pictures given in Scripture that indicate what believers will have in heaven—terms like "crowns", "streets of gold," or being "co-heirs who will reign with Christ." But here Paul was not calling believers to simply count their heavenly money this side of eternity; rather, he was longing for these believers to grasp that, in God, they had everything! They had indescribable wealth in light of the fact that everything glorious awaited them in heaven—guaranteed (see Matt. 13:46; 1 Peter 1:4). Believers now and forever can know they are rich toward God (see Luke 12:21).[21]

Last, Paul wanted them to gain the conviction that they had an incredible resource in the Lord. In verse 19 he described the believer's access to the Lord's *inexhaustible power*. He wanted them to know "… what is the immeasurable greatness of his power toward us who believe, according to the working of his great might." He heaped six descriptive terms one on top of the other to describe this immense power of God. Each word overlaps the other, creating a cumulative picture of God's exceeding power and strength. The first three words are found in the phrase "immeasurable greatness of his power." This combination of terms conveys the idea of something that is beyond possible understanding. Trying to understand God's power is like trying to follow a ballistic missile that has been launched. God's power surpasses, or exceeds, all greatness in terms of size. It is more than any and all other forms of power.

The last three descriptive terms regarding this power are found in the phrase "… according to the working of his great might." Paul painted a glorious picture of what this church had—and all Christians have—access to. He showed the power as operative, energized, and strong. When he depicted this power as being "according to … his great might," he uniquely connected what believers have to its source—God himself. In essence, the nature of this power is aligned with the very nature of God. This is enemy-crushing, tide-turning power like that of a victorious king over an enemy in battle. God is mighty, ensuring that his power will accomplish all his objectives. There is no better example regarding the power Christians have from God than the one he chooses: that this power is the same that resurrected and enthroned Jesus at the Father's right hand, over all creation, and over God's beloved church (Eph. 1:20–23).

To be illumined by this power is to see these concepts as concretely as if seeing "... a bulldozer [having] the ability, capacity, and potential of routing out trees. By looking at it, one senses its inherent strength but when its engine roars and it begins to move, its power of mastery becomes obvious."[22] Paul's logic here was simple: Because they were saved, they were illumined. And because they had been illumined, they needed to grasp these three key concepts—salvation's guarantee, wealth, and power. To truly be illumined to know these truths is extraordinary.

The idea that Paul was praying for this church to be illumined regarding spiritual realities is threaded through the epistle of Ephesians. Chapter 3 introduces what could be seen as Paul's second prayer, in which he prayed that the Ephesian believers would know the rich love they had received in Christ. In Ephesians 3:16–19, he asked that they would be "strengthened with power through his Spirit in [their] inner being, so that Christ may dwell in [their] hearts through faith," and that they "may have strength to ... know the love of Christ that surpasses knowledge, that [they] may be filled with all the fullness of God" (vv. 3:16–19). Paul prayed that God, according to his rich glory, would illumine their inner being so that by faith they would grasp the deep, deep love of Jesus. In verse 19, Paul said that this love "surpasses knowledge." He was readily admitting that, from a strictly human or superficial standpoint, the Ephesians would not be able to understand this love; grasping this kind of divine love in this way, at this level, necessitates the work of the Spirit. This is beyond mere human thinking—it necessitates illumined thinking.

What is interesting to note is how Paul characterized this work of God as being "filled with all the fullness of God." Paul used "fullness" throughout the book of Ephesians, each time in reference to a spiritual dimension. At 1:23, Jesus, as the head of the church, was said to be "the fullness of him who fills all in all," the life-giving source as the head over his body. As we have seen, 3:19 was Paul's prayer for believers to be spiritually "filled with all the fullness of God." Paul later addressed this again, commanding believers to "be filled with the Spirit" (5:18).

The context of the book sheds light on this command. In Ephesians 4:1, Paul exhorted the believers in their daily Christian living, calling them to "walk in a manner worthy of [their] calling." The idea here was that this church could fall prey to the influences that surrounded them in the worldly society of Ephesus. Immorality and idol worship were two main components of the city's reputation, and Paul's concern was for the Ephesians' holiness—that they not slip back into former sinful habits that characterized their lives prior to their becoming believers. In Ephesians 5:17–18, Paul challenged them to flee their former party lifestyles and instead to pursue God's will. Specifically, Paul said that, instead of being "foolish," they needed to "understand what the will of the Lord is" (5:17), and then restated this in saying, "do not get drunk with wine ... but be filled with the Spirit" (5:18). There are many interpretations of what it means for a believer to "be filled with the Spirit," but one key pointer has to be that Paul again used the word "filled." Both of Paul's prayers in this letter (Eph. 1:15–23 and Eph. 3:14–21) were for these believers to be illumined, to know or understand spiritual truths, and the commands in 5:17–18 should be understood as the church's way to respond.

Though illumination is the Spirit's work in the heart of a believer, this command shows that believers are still responsible to yield themselves to this work. In fact, in Ephesians 5:17–18, three of the four commands are in the passive voice: "do not be foolish," "do not get drunk," and "be filled with the Spirit" (the Greek literally says, "be filled *in* Spirit"). This points to the atmosphere of the believer's thinking, emphasizing the necessity for believers to yield themselves to the Spirit's work in their lives. In verse 17, Paul called them to actively "understand" God's will for holiness, and then calls believers to submit their hearts to being "filled with the Spirit." This filling can be understood as the believer yielding him- or herself to the Spirit's work of illumination (compare Ps. 119:18).

In Philippians 1:9 Paul similarly prayed that the love of the church in Philippi would "... abound more and more, with knowledge and all discernment"; and again, in Colossians 1:9, he prayed that the church in Colosse would "... be filled with the knowledge of his will in all spiritual wisdom and understanding." This was an often-repeated desire Paul had for the church at large. As in Ephesians, Paul's prayer for the Colossians took on a practical dimension in Colossians 3. Having prayed for this church to gain "knowledge" and "spiritual wisdom"—again, synonymous with the work of illumination—Paul put legs on this request, exhorting believers to actively "seek the things that are above, where Christ is" (Col. 3:1) and then to "Let the word of Christ dwell in you richly" (Col. 3:16). Both commands emphasize the role believers are to take in being illumined. Paul directed believers to focus their minds on biblical content—here, "the word of Christ" (Col. 3:16). As with the Ephesians, believers were illumined for the express purpose of gaining spiritual convictions, which came when the Spirit impressed the truths of God's Word in greater depth, creating greater certainty.

PETER

The apostle Peter, like Paul, emphasized a great confidence in the Word as the agent by which a person is illumined. Peter wrote some of the clearest teaching in all of the New Testament on this subject in 2 Peter 1. Sensing that the end of his life was drawing near (2 Peter 1:14), Peter wanted the churches in his charge to be secure. Although he recognized that these Christians were "established in the truth" (1:12), he made no apologies about restating what they knew, "by way of reminder" (1:13), so that they would be able to recall it after he was gone (1:15). What he said was comprised of two parts: Peter first recounted his experience with Christ on the Mount of Transfiguration (see Matt. 17:1–8), then he gave a higher endorsement for the Word of God. He wrote in 2 Peter 1:16–21,

For we did not follow cleverly devised myths when we made known to you the power and coming of our Lord Jesus Christ, but we were eyewitnesses of his majesty. For when he received honor and glory from God the Father, and the voice was borne to him by the Majestic Glory, "This is my beloved Son, with whom I am well pleased," we ourselves heard this very voice borne from heaven, for we were with him on the holy mountain. And we have something more sure, the prophetic word, to which you will do well to pay attention as to a lamp shining in a dark place, until the day dawns and the morning star rises in your hearts, knowing this first of all, that no prophecy of Scripture comes from someone's own interpretation. For no prophecy was ever produced by the will of man, but men spoke from God as they were carried along by the Holy Spirit.

Peter recounted the experience he, James, and John had when they saw the glory and power of Christ firsthand, which was followed by hearing God the Father's voice of affirmation. This was an unparalleled experience. However, instead of holding this experience up as his authority, in verse 19 he wrote of "something more sure" than this incredible experience: "the prophetic word."

Peter testified to having heard directly from God, but affirmed a higher testimony—a "more sure … prophetic word" that is illumined to each and every believer's heart by the Spirit. He esteemed the objective revelation of the Word of God above the experiential revelation of the transfigured Christ. Peter was making the point that, barring Christ's return in their lifetime, his readers would never see Christ's glory in that way, yet they were still on solid ground. Their certainty came from their confidence in the Word that had been illumined to their hearts. Peter likened illumination to "… a lamp shining in a dark place" and the dawning of the day when "… the morning star rises in [believers'] hearts" (1:19).

This experience of illumination resonates with every believer. Peter elevated Scripture above experience as the means for knowing God. This means that the same illumination he had can be had by all believers—even those of us who will not see the risen Christ until we arrive in heaven. Peter brought everything back to Scripture and reminds us that Scripture originated from "the Holy Spirit" (1:21). As a fitting conclusion to his epistle, he offered his final prayer that these believers would mature in their spiritual convictions, exhorting them to "… grow in the grace and knowledge of our Lord and Savior Jesus Christ" (3:18).

JOHN

The last author we will examine here is the apostle John. John made reference to the necessity of illumination in protecting believers from heretical teaching. John, like Peter, was advanced in years and coming to the end of his ministry as he wrote the book of 1 John. Over and over again he referred to those under his shepherding care as "my little children" (see, for example, 1 John 2:1). Out of a desire to guard and protect his flock, he warned them of the false teachers, who were people in the church and whom he called "antichrists" (2:18). They were those who denied "that Jesus is the Christ," ultimately denying "the Father and the Son" (2:22). John affirmed that the believers whom he shepherded and loved had "been anointed ... and [had] knowledge," so they were able to combat these heresies (2:20).

The concept of being anointed comes directly from the Old Testament priesthood. Anointing was a symbolic ceremony whereby priests were set apart from the rest of Israel as those who would carry out an intercessory ministry between the nation and God. The primary example of this was the Aaronic priesthood, in which men were designated to perform the ceremonial duties (Exod. 30:30). In Old Testament history, Israel's kings were also anointed (1 Sam. 16:12), symbolizing their significant role as those separated by God to act as his spokesmen, intercessors, and mediators as they ruled God's nation. To be anointed meant being covered with oil. This conveyed that the anointed person was owned by the LORD and was consecrated for the LORD's use. As we saw earlier, Christ quoted Isaiah 61:1, saying of himself, "The Spirit of the Lord is upon me, because he has anointed me to proclaim good news to the poor" (Luke 4:18). Jesus was not referring here to a physical anointing, but to the Spirit's illuminating work to empower him "to proclaim" the gospel.

By understanding the foundation of the ceremony of anointing from the Old Testament it becomes clearer what John meant in 1 John as he expanded this picture to a spiritual anointing for all believers. This anointing, instead of covering the outer skin, is dealing with the inner man. John wrote in 1 John 2:20–21 of believers in the church, "But you have been anointed by the Holy One, and you all have knowledge. I write to you, not because you do not know the truth, but because you know it, and because no lie is of the truth." Note that the anointing is connected with "knowledge" (2:20) and that the believers "know it" (2:21). As with the Old Testament symbol, believers are set apart, but now it is their *minds* that are set apart—to the truth.

This goes back to our main point. John affirmed that believers have illumined spiritual convictions, what he called "knowledge" (1 John 2:20).

For those to whom he wrote, and for all believers, these convictions serve to protect against false teachers and false teaching. Believers are not solely dependent upon spiritually gifted teachers in the church to interpret the meaning of Scripture (1 John 2:27). Though gifted teachers are part of what makes a church strong, edified and protected (1 Cor. 12:28; Eph. 4:11; 1 Tim. 3:2), it is the anointing of the Spirit of God that is the guide to truth. This anointing can and should be likened to the burning convictions that were born in the two disciples on the road to Emmaus.

Implications for the preacher

There is no better evaluative gauge for a person's spiritual condition than his or her spiritual convictions. These are the byproducts of illumination. Convictions are mile-markers for growth. The preacher should evaluate himself according to the spiritual convictions he has gained in his study of Scripture. Without possessing these, how can he ever expect anything to happen in the hearts of his flock when he preaches? These convictions are resident in a soul that is illumined to see "… the glory of all the perfections of God and of everything appertaining to the divine Being."[23] The heart that is converted is never content to sit dormant, to remain unmoved throughout life only to quicken in glory. Instead, once energized by the Spirit and truth, the heart gives birth to an appetite, whereby a follower of Christ continues to grow, hungry throughout life for illumined truth. For there to be real health in a church, both preachers and hearers need to examine themselves, asking, "When was the last time I sensed the burning conviction that the Scripture I heard or read is truth?"

Notes

1 **Greg Heisler,** *Spirit-Led Preaching: The Holy Spirit's Role in Sermon Preparation and Delivery* (Nashville: B & H Academic, 2007), p. 46.
2 **Bernard L. Ramm,** *Rapping about the Spirit* (Waco, TX: Word, 1974), p. 84.
3 Ibid.
4 Ibid.
5 Ibid.

6   **John Calvin,** "Geneva Catechism," in **Thomas F. Torrance,** (ed. and tr.), *The School of Faith: The Catechisms of the Reformed Church* (Eugene, OR: Wipf and Stock, 1959), pp. 52–53.

7   **John Calvin, John T. McNeill,** (ed.), and **Ford Lewis Battles** (tr.), *Calvin: Institutes of the Christian Religion*, vols. XX and XXI of **John Baillie, John T. McNeill,** and **Henry P. Van Dusen,** (eds.), *The Library of Christian Classics* (Louisville, KY: Westminster John Knox Press, 1960), p. 79.

8   Ibid. p. 80.

9   **Kevin J. Vanhoozer,** *Is There a Meaning in This Text? The Bible, the Reader, and the Morality of Literary Knowledge* (Grand Rapids, MI: Zondervan, 1998), p. 413.

10 Heisler, *Spirit-Led Preaching*, p. 43. Heisler's definition is based upon the work of Robert H. Stein in his book *Playing by the Rules: A Basic Guide to Interpreting the Bible* (Grand Rapids, MI: Baker, 1994).

11 **Charles Hodge,** *Commentary on the Second Epistle to the Corinthians* (1864; n.d., Grand Rapids, MI: Eerdmans), p. 91.

12 **George J. Zemek,** *The Word of God in the Child of God: Exegetical, Theological, and Homiletical Reflections from the 119th Psalm* (Mango, FL: n.p.; n.d.), p. 103.

13 **Jonathan Edwards,** *The Religious Affections* (1746; 1986, Carlisle, PA: Banner of Truth), p. 194.

14 Ibid. p. 198.

15 Ibid. pp. 195–196.

16 Ibid. p. 197.

17 I take it this way because "spirit" is anarthrous, that is, it has no definite article, unlike in verse 13, where "the Spirit" is clearly the third member of the Trinity.

18 **John Calvin, T. H. L. Parker,** (tr.), *The Epistles of Paul the Apostle to the Galatians, Ephesians, Philippians and Colossians*, vol. ii of **David W. Torrance** and **Thomas F. Torrance,** (eds.), *Calvin's New Testament Commentaries* (Grand Rapids, MI: Eerdmans, 1965), p. 134.

19 **Homer A Kent, Jr.,** *Ephesians: The Glory of the Church* (Everyman's Bible Commentary; Chicago: Moody Press, 1971), p. 29.

20 **Charles Hodge,** *Ephesians* (The Geneva Series of Commentaries; 1856; 1991, Carlisle, PA: Banner of Truth, 1991), p. 41.

21 I use the phrase "rich toward God" to refer to spiritually minded people as opposed to unspiritually minded people, whom Jesus condemns in Luke 12:21. Jesus, in that context, condemns those who are covetous, saying they are "not rich toward God," in contrast to

people who are "rich toward God" and who by faith live for the "riches" and "inheritance" that await them in heaven.

22 Harold Hoehner, *Ephesians: An Exegetical Commentary* (Grand Rapids, MI: Baker Academic, 2002), p. 271.

23 Edwards, *The Religious Affections*, p. 199.

Conclusion

Without a biblical gauge, there is no credible way in which to evaluate whether or not preaching is making an authentic difference for the glory of God. It is important to have biblical expectations from a biblical framework in order to understand the effect the Word is to have as it is preached. I have presented these four categories in the hope that they will build just such a grid to shape the expectations for preachers and for hearers.

It is typical that a preacher today does not think biblically about how to evaluate his preaching ministry. Too often, an extra-biblical measuring stick, such as "attendance" or "offerings," is used to gauge success. This can lead to preachers becoming performance-based in the pulpit, all because the Holy Spirit's promised ministry of illumination is undervalued or simply forgotten. Illumination is missing in preaching because it is missing in the preacher. When the Holy Spirit's role is divorced from personal study, this naturally affects the pulpit, and thus the hearers.

Sometimes a preacher looks for the Holy Spirit to come and bless his speaking ability apart from blessing the Word as it is proclaimed. What happens when this extra blessing of the Spirit does not appear? The preacher may become confused and discouraged. This kind of subjective evaluation of preaching leaves out the Spirit's role of illumining the preached Word. Regrettably, many books on the Holy Spirit reinforce this kind of subjectivity by completely skipping over the theme of illumination as it pertains to the pastor's study and pulpit. Again, the clear concern is a lack of biblical expectations for both preacher and preaching, for the private study and public ministry.

Regardless of a preacher's platform or phase of ministry, confidence in communicating rises or falls based on the expectation of what preaching will accomplish. A clear understanding of illumination will, like a fresh breeze, offer a renewed sense of confidence in disciplined exegetical study coupled with energetic, affectionate, expositional preaching. It will change the preacher. This God-inspired and God-blessed work of illumination can turn study into worship. No longer is study mere preparation to speak, it is worship of Jesus. Understood and prioritized correctly, preaching becomes the overflow of what has first happened in the preacher's heart and mind. This kind of preaching connects the ministry of the Spirit with the Word of God, reinvigorating both study and pulpit.

There is such a noteworthy difference in sermon preparation when it is approached with biblical expectations in mind, and the four categories we have outlined can become a framework for developing right biblical expectations. They can prompt many questions, such as, "What is going to happen when I preach?"; "Is the Holy Spirit stirring my affections while I study, pray, and meditate?"; "Will the Lord save somebody from hell when I preach this time?"; "Will someone become angry or bitter and reject what I am going to say?"; "Will someone's spiritual life be refreshed as he or she takes another spiritual step toward being like Jesus?" Questions like these reflect a heart that is beginning to understand the dynamic of illumination in preparation, preaching, and hearing.

An example from the apostle Paul's preaching ministry may be the best way to illustrate these biblical expectations. This episode contains the four categories of illumination we have outlined, linking a right view of illumination with a right view of preaching. In Acts 17, Paul, having taught the resurrection of Jesus in the synagogues in Athens, was compelled by Epicurean and Stoic philosophers to take this message to a different forum: Mars Hill. Paul took a different approach with this audience as he preached the resurrection of Jesus and called those listening to repent (vv. 30–31). See the various ways in which those present responded: "Now when they heard of the resurrection of the dead, some mocked. But others said, 'We will hear you again about this.' So Paul went out from their midst. But some men joined him and believed, among whom also were Dionysius the Areopagite and a woman named Damaris and others with them" (vv. 32–34).

Here the four categories of illumination can be seen. First, based on Paul's *communication* of the Word, people responded. The way God designed for these hearers to be challenged was through preaching. Paul gave an impassioned delivery, saying, "What therefore you worship as unknown, this I *proclaim* to you" (v. 23).

Second, the preaching of the Word brought some under *condemnation.*

There were those who overtly rejected the gospel—"some mocked." People who make fun of the Word of God are in a very sobering and dangerous place. They are not unlike the crowds who mocked Jesus while he was dying on the cross and who, at the end, will be found scoffing and mocking Jesus's return (2 Peter 3:3–4). These ungodly ones will be destroyed by the very Lord they mock (2 Peter 3:7).

Third, some were illumined and some, saying "We will hear you again," were what Owen called "pre-illumined."[1] Though still unregenerate, these are people Jesus might have characterized as he did a certain scribe, saying, "You are not far from the kingdom of God" (Mark 12:34). Those who were asking for more teaching can be placed along with those who "joined him [Paul] and believed" under the category of *conversion*. They were seeking the light, and were on the cusp of regeneration, which is where illumination begins.

Fourth, the words "joined and believed" can be read as a strong confirmation of these men and this woman—assuming, for the sake of this work, that those who joined Paul as committed followers would be gaining *convictions* as they grew in grace and in the knowledge of Jesus and his Word (see 2 Peter 3:18).

With these biblical expectations in mind, how ought the preacher to approach preaching? While there is no exact formula to ensure Spirit-illumined preaching, there are two clear steps that a preacher must take while he prepares his text for clarity. First, the preacher must pray for God's Spirit to illumine his mind in the study, just as the psalmist prayed (Ps. 119:18) and the apostle Paul prayed for believers to be illumined (see Chapter 6: Convictions through Illumination). Here the communicator realizes his absolute need for the Spirit's intervention as he casts himself upon God in complete reliance. Here is an example of this prayer in study: "Lord, please make the Scripture clear to me so I can present the truth in an understandable way, so that people will come away spiritually awakened and affected by it."

Second, the preacher must meditate. He must move beyond academics to a deep consideration of his biblical passage: what it meant when it was originally written, what it means for his own life personally, and finally what it means for his people. Meditation is the time when the Spirit of God grabs a heart with his Word—convincing the believer of the text's veracity and convicting of sin. Meditation should result in a preacher gaining convictions and deep abiding affections over the profound significance of the text to be preached. Once illumined, the preacher's role is to convey those truths to his hearers while maintaining a deep reliance upon the text he is preaching, in the hope that the Spirit of God will likewise illumine the hearts of his hearers through the agency of the Word preached, creating deep convictions, spiritual growth, and greater depth and height of worship.

Instead of relying on academic minutiae, contrived mystical effects, pragmatic manipulations, or even homiletical abilities, the preacher must see the need for the Holy Spirit to sweep him up as he pores over his text each week in heartfelt prayer and meditation with the hope that those who listen will consequently be swept up as well. Though there may come seasons of dryness in study and preaching, this study of illumination clearly reveals that boldness in preaching is generated from convictions impressed on a heart that has been illumined from texts studied, and that these Spirit-wrought biblical convictions translate into empowered, impassioned, and ignited sermons.

The preacher should never exchange the time and discipline necessary for exegetical study for time spent in prayer and meditation, but must make a way for both of these elements. John Owen, who contributed what may be the essential theological treatment of the doctrine of illumination, documented this crucial harmony of disciplines: "… the means of the right interpretation of the Scripture, and understanding the mind of God therein, are of two sorts,—first, such as prescribed unto us in a way of duty, as *prayer, meditation* on the word itself, and the like; and, secondly, *disciplinary*, in the accommodation of *arts and sciences*, with all kind of learning, unto that work …"[2]

Owen's words reiterate that the reason why the preacher must carefully exegete his passage is to clearly understand it and, in turn, to accurately present it (see 2 Tim. 2:15). Once clarity is gained through prayer and disciplined study, the preacher can effectively and easily ponder his text, meditating so as to be gripped by the implications of it as he is illumined by God's Spirit. Bible scholar Dr. Bernard L. Ramm depicts this very clearly in two illustrations borrowed from Danish philosopher and existentialist Søren Kierkegaard:

Kierkegaard poses the question how a lover reads a love letter from his lover when they happen to speak two different languages. The first thing the lover must do with the letter is to translate it. He gets out his dictionary of the foreign language—perhaps even a grammar—and goes to work. He translates it word by word, line by line, paragraph by paragraph, until the entire translated letter is on the desk before him.

But doing all that hard work of translating that letter into his language is not to read the letter as a love letter. Now that he has the complete translation he relaxes, leans back in his chair, and reads the translated letter as a love letter.

So it is with the Holy Scripture. We cannot avoid all the hard work of looking up Hebrew and Greek words, puzzling over constructions, consulting commentaries, and other such helps. But doing this careful academic job of translating and interpreting Scripture is not to read the Word of God as the Word of God … But to read the Scripture as the Word of God he must read it the second time. Now it is no longer an academic task but it is a case of letting God's Word get through to a man's soul as *God's Word*. It is in the second reading of the letter that the Holy Spirit … enters into the process of understanding Holy Scripture.

Kierkegaard gives a second illustration. A little boy is to be spanked by his father. While the father goes for the rod the boy stuffs the bottom of his pants with several table napkins. When the father returns and administers the whipping the boys feels no pain as the napkins absorb the whack of the rod. The little boy represents the biblical scholars. They pad their britches with their lexicons, commentaries, and concordances. As a result the Scripture never reaches them as the Word of God. Having nullified its power by shielding themselves with their academic paraphernalia, they thus never hear the Scriptures as the Word of God. If they would unpack their books from their britches (which are necessary rightfully used, as illustrated in the story of the love letter) then the Scriptures could get through to them as the Word of God. Allowing Holy Scripture to get through to us as the Word of God is the special work of the Holy Spirit.[3]

Moving from expectations for study, what kind of expectations ought the preacher to have for illumination in preaching? The apostle Paul stands out as a superb example. His testimony as a preacher to the Thessalonians was simple. He reminded them in no uncertain terms that "… our gospel came to you not only in word, but also in power and in the Holy Spirit and with full conviction. You know what kind of men we proved to be among you for your sake" (1 Thes. 1:5). Paul's preaching was authentic. Why? Because it was the Word of God empowered by the Spirit of God, and it burst from his illumined heart "with full conviction!" Illumination starts in the study but the Spirit's role of illumining the heart is also necessary in the pulpit. The preacher stands as a humble vessel ready for God's Word to pour from his mouth, and the deep impressions of the truths studied are pressed even deeper into his heart as he declares them. Like Paul, he simply believes and so speaks (see the chapter on Conviction and 2 Cor. 4:13). This dynamic is what makes preaching unique and powerful. Being illumined while preaching is how illumined convictions are passed from the communicator to the listener as the listener hears with spiritual ears. Owen explained the crucial reason why the preacher must seek to be illumined:

And there is not any truth of greater importance for men to be established in; for unless they have a *full assurance of understanding in themselves*, unless they hold their persuasion of the sense of Scripture revelations from God alone, if their spiritual judgment of truth and falsehood depend on the authority of men, they will never be able to undergo any suffering for the truth or to perform any duty unto God in a right manner.4

This "inward persuasion of the Holy Spirit" is what gave martyrs of old strength to give their lives for the gospel.5 This blood earnestness should be no different for the preacher in the pulpit. Illumined preaching flows from the illumined preacher—the preacher who is convinced that the stakes of pastoral duty are eternal; this man preaches a message he is willing to die for.

And what of the hearers? What ought the preacher to expect of them? The preacher who is ministering with wrong expectations can be emotionally tossed up and down as if in a turbulent sea by his perceived successes and failures in preaching. Right biblical expectations will not only inform but hopefully also resuscitate discouraged preachers. The Spirit's promised ministry has been there all along. Some will hear and have hearts illumined by the Spirit to believe, understand, and grow in spiritual convictions. Others will hear, reject, and remain under condemnation. The preacher must expect that, whatever the outcome, whatever God's purpose, God will be glorified.

Let us make this more personal, and hopefully very practical. What does this mean for us and our preaching ministries? What should we expect when we preach? As Spirit-filled preachers we should assume that the Lord will illumine our minds both in the study and during the preaching event. Listen to the way Carl Hargrove described this balance in his thesis on the Spirit's role in preaching:

It is … a reasonable, if not a necessary conclusion, that the Spirit *does* illumine the mind in preaching, since He does in the interpretive process. Illuminational preaching is that which depends on the Spirit to take the effort of exegesis and, according to the Spirit's sovereign plan, make those thoughts cogent in the mind of the preacher—he experiences what the Psalmist longed to experience [see Ps. 119:18, 25, 27, and 31], yet in a different context—the preaching event. It would include insight that is beyond the preacher's normal giftedness and abilities, and a freedom to express these thoughts in a manner that is most edifying to his listeners. Illuminational preaching includes bringing the truth of Scripture to bear in the minds of the audience.[6]

Also, the apostles who were commissioned by Christ to preach likewise anticipated the promise that they would be Spirit-illumined after Jesus was gone. In this way, the apostles served as forerunners for all illumined preaching since. Their ministry was obviously very similar to and yet very different from that of today's preacher. Hargrove clarified the distinctions:

What the apostles experienced was both illuminational and revelational—their minds were enlightened to remember truths of the Scriptures and the ministry of Christ as promised by the Lord (John 14:26); they were channels for revelation, which would be moved from oral to written record. For post-apostolic preaching, the mind of the minister is *still and only illumined* to the truths of Scripture, and the mind of the listener is illumined to the truth of the message.[7]

This being the case, we ought to expect within our minds an illumined dynamic whereby we gain more and more conviction and affection over the text during delivery. Dr. Albert Mohler affirmed this, recognizing that preachers are instruments who "speak what He Himself [God] has spoken ... through the preaching of Scripture under the illumination and *testimonium* of the Holy Spirit."[8]

What of our hearers? Knowing that it is ultimately the Lord who gives life or death (conversion or condemnation) as we preach might tempt us to take a passive attitude. This would be unbiblical and lacking the integrity demanded by our calling. D. Martyn Lloyd-Jones said,

Do you expect anything to happen when you get up to preach in a pulpit? Or do you just say to yourself, "Well, I have prepared my address, I am going to give them this address; some of them will appreciate it and some will not?" Are you expecting it to be the turning point in someone's life? Are you expecting anyone to have a climactic experience? That is what preaching is meant to do.[9]

In the mystery of God, instead of being passive or blasé, we are called to see ourselves as a means by which the Lord brings eternal life (1 Tim. 4:16).

With this in mind, let us expect nothing less of ourselves than to prepare and deliver clear, authentic, enlivened, heart-affected truth with people's souls in view. Let us expect that some will gain deeper and higher Spirit-given convictions as they hear God's Spirit-inspired text. At the same time, expect that some will hear the Word of God and reject it as foolishness, only to continue as blind men and women down a path toward condemnation. Understanding this balance may keep us from spiritual pride and a holier-than-thou attitude. As Paul said, "For we are the aroma of Christ to God among those who are being saved and among those who are perishing, to one a fragrance from death to death, to the other a fragrance from life to life. Who is sufficient for these things?" (2 Cor. 2:15–16).

Paul's attitude toward his preaching was anything but resigned or passive. He felt the highs and lows, and he had a real grip on the eternal stakes of his ministry—that people either gained life or were condemned. He was God-centered. Paul knew he was an instrument and only that; he was God's vessel for pouring out his Word on people. Paul was no different from preachers who have gone before or after him. Whether we look at the prophets or the Son of God himself, the results of illumined preaching are the same. Whether we evaluate Calvin, Luther, Owen, or Edwards, the results of illumined preaching are the same. Why should we expect anything different? The blind will see, the deaf will hear, and some will reject.

So, what is our admonition? Preach the Word—but only after having first been illumined by it. Then, with a clear conscience, preach, expecting those listening to gain convictions, illumined convictions, the Bible's convictions. This is authentic biblical communication. We preach as messengers, shepherds, and soldiers, ever persevering in our calling and duty with the knowledge that people will both accept and reject the Word of God. The Bible sets this agenda—it is our acid test for how we are doing. This is what makes our backbones strong and our confidence sure in what the Holy Spirit will accomplish through his truth proclaimed. This blessed ministry of the Spirit "… may rightly be called the *key* that unlocks for us the treasures of the Kingdom of Heaven [see Rev. 3:7]; and his illumination, the keenness of our insight."[10]

Notes

1 **John Owen,** *The Holy Spirit: His Gifts and Power* (Grand Rapids, MI: Kregel, 1954), pp. 135–138.

2 **John Owen, William H. Goold,** (ed.), *The Works of John Owen*, vol. iv (1850; 1967, London: Banner of Truth), p. 126.

3 **Bernard L. Ramm,** *Rapping about the Spirit* (Waco, TX: Word, 1974), pp. 85–86. See **Søren Kierkegaard,** and **Howard V. Hong** and **Edna H. Hong,** (tr. and eds.), *For Self-Examination* in *Kierkegaard's Writings*, vol. xxi (1851; 1990, Princeton: Princeton University Press), pp. 26–35.

4 **Owen,** *Works*, p. 123.

5 **John Calvin,** and **John T. McNeill,** (ed.), and **Ford Lewis Battles,** (tr.), *Calvin: Institutes of*

the *Christian Religion*, vols. xx and xxi of **John Baillie, John T. McNeill,** and **Henry P. Van Dusen,** (eds.), *The Library of Christian Classics* (Louisville, KY: Westminster John Knox Press, 1960), p. 92.

6 **Carl A. Hargrove,** "The Role of the Holy Spirit as Convictor and Supporter in Preaching," Master's thesis, The Master's Seminary, 2006, p. 115.

7 Ibid. p. 114.

8 **Albert Mohler,** "Why Do We Preach? A Foundation for Christian Preaching, Part One," December 15, 2005, "Commentary," at: AlbertMohler.com.

9 **D. Martyn Lloyd-Jones,** *Preaching and Preachers* (1971; 1985, London: Hodder and Stoughton), p. 325.

10 **Calvin,** *Institutes*, p. 542.

This Appendix contains the results of my study of key words related to the Holy Spirit's work of illumining the minds of people throughout the Bible. (See Chapter 1 for further explanation.) References are listed in canonical order. They are followed by summary explanations and are categorized as either *direct* or *indirect* (sometimes by implication) references to illumination.

Three charts follow the list of references. The first addresses the issue of how directly the Bible speaks of the doctrine of illumination in both Old and New Testaments. The second simply shows that the bulk of revelation regarding this theological subject is in the New Testament. The third chart shows a breakdown of references to illumination by genre or author.

Old Testament

PENTATEUCH
Genesis 41:38–39   Moses, the author of Genesis, made an early reference to the Spirit of God providing man with discernment and wisdom. Joseph was commended by Pharaoh for possessing this discernment and wisdom, having been gifted to interpret Pharaoh's dreams. This is a *direct* reference to illumination.

Exodus 31:1–6; 35:30–33   Moses, the author of Exodus, recorded that Bezalel, a son from the tribe of Judah, was filled with the Spirit of God, which enabled him to skillfully and intelligently create Israel's tabernacle furniture. This is a *direct* reference to illumination, as the Spirit of God informs a person's mind to know the LORD's will and how to carry it out.

Numbers 11:16–17, 24–29   Moses, the author of Numbers, recorded how the LORD put some of the Spirit on seventy of the elders of Israel for them to prophesy. The Spirit of God enabled these seventy elders to communicate revelation. This is an *indirect* reference to illumination by implication, because Moses did not record the seventy understanding revelation in this section.

Numbers 24:1   Moses recorded that Balaam, upon whom the Spirit of

God came and gave him an oracle to speak, opened his eyes to see and his ears to hear and understand the message from the LORD. This is a *direct* reference to illumination, as the Spirit of God opened Balaam's mind to God's Word.

Numbers 27:16–18   Joshua is identified as a man in whom the Spirit of God resides. This, by implication, is an *indirect* reference to illumination whereby Joshua, by means of the Spirit, could spiritually understand revelation.

Deuteronomy 4:9   Moses, the author of Deuteronomy, exhorted the children of Israel to keep careful watch over their souls, remembering what God had revealed to them. God's revelation of himself, whether by word or deed, was on the heart of the nation Israel. This, by *implication*, means Israel had been illumined to see God's revelation.

Deuteronomy 17:18–19   Israel's kings wrote and read the Law of God to learn to fear the LORD. This, by implication, is an *indirect* reference to illumination, and means that kings were illumined by God's law to fear the LORD.

Deuteronomy 34:9   Joshua was full of the spirit of wisdom, which implies that he, as the leader of Israel, was illumined by the Spirit of God. This is an *indirect* reference to illumination.

HISTORY BOOKS

1 Samuel 3:7   Samuel had not yet been illumined through the Word of the LORD because it had not been revealed to him up to this point. This is a *direct* reference to illumination.

1 Samuel 10:6, 10   The Spirit of the LORD rushed upon Saul, enabling him to speak prophecies. This is an *indirect* reference to illumination, by which the Spirit of the LORD enables a person to speak revelation, implying that he can understand revelation.

1 Samuel 19:20–23   The Spirit of God enabled not only Saul but also other prophets to speak revelation. This is an *indirect* reference to illumination, by which the Spirit of the LORD enables a person to speak revelation, implying that he can understand revelation.

2 Samuel 7:27   David affirms that God has revealed truth to him, and on that basis he was courageous to pray. This is a *direct* reference to illumination, by which God reveals truth directly to his servant.

2 Samuel 23:1–3   David testified that the Spirit of the LORD spoke to him. Through illumination, David had ready access to know and speak God's Word. This is a *direct* reference to illumination.

1 Kings 3:9–12; 4:29–32   God granted Solomon's request for understanding, wisdom, and discernment. Solomon's mind was enhanced by the work of God, and he was able to be an effective king over Israel. Solomon was enabled to lead wisely and to write biblical proverbs. This is an *indirect* reference to illumination where, by implication, the Spirit of God enabled Solomon to understand, be wise, and possess discernment.

1 Kings 22:21–24   God gave a lying spirit to false prophets. This is the antithesis of God's gift of his Spirit to enable understanding and to speak truth. This, by antithesis, is an *indirect* reference to illumination.

1 Chronicles 12:17–18   The Spirit of the LORD clothed Amasai, empowering him to prophesy. This affirmed the loyalty of the Benjamites and Judahites to David, who was king over Israel. This is an *indirect* reference to illumination, where, by implication, the Spirit of God enabled men to prophesy God's revelation.

1 Chronicles 22:12   David expresses his deep desire for his son Solomon to be given discretion and understanding as Israel's next king. Solomon's being granted discretion and understanding correlates with David's desire for Solomon to obey the law of the LORD. This is an *indirect* reference to illumination, where, by implication, the Spirit of God would enable Solomon to understand and be faithful to the law of the LORD.

1 Chronicles 27:32   Jonathan was affirmed as a man of understanding. This is an *indirect* reference to illumination as this man's gaining understanding was predicated on the Spirit of God's enabling.

2 Chronicles 18:20–23   A lying spirit given by God to false prophets is the antithesis of God giving his Spirit to enable understanding and speak truth. This, by antithesis, is an *indirect* reference to illumination.

2 Chronicles 20:14–15   The Spirit of the LORD provided a Levite revelation in the form of prophecy. This is an *indirect* reference to illumination, where, by implication, Jahaziel was given revelation by the Spirit.

2 Chronicles 24:20   The Spirit of God clothed Zechariah, giving him revelation to prophesy. This is an *indirect* reference to illumination, in which Zechariah's understanding of the revelation is implied.

2 Chronicles 36:22–23   God stirred up the spirit of Cyrus, which is synonymous to Cyrus being stirred in his mind. This is an *indirect* reference to illumination, whereby Cyrus was given understanding of revelation to make proclamation and record revelation.

Ezra 1:1–2   God stirred up the spirit of Cyrus, which is synonymous to Cyrus being stirred in his mind. This is an *indirect* reference to illumination, whereby Cyrus was given understanding of revelation to make proclamation and record revelation.

Nehemiah 8:2–3   When Ezra preached, the ears of Israel were attentive to the Word of the LORD—the Law. This is an *indirect* reference to illumination; the reference to the people's attentiveness could imply that they were spiritually illumined.

Nehemiah 9:20   Ezra recounted God's faithfulness to Israel in that he gave them his Spirit, enabling them to know revelation. This is a *direct* reference to illumination.

Nehemiah 9:30   By the Spirit of God, Israel was warned through prophets. They were not given the grace of illumination as they rejected prophetic word. This is an *indirect* reference to illumination, and specifically the rejection of Spirit-led prophecy.

Nehemiah 10:28   Certain people of Israel—those separated to the Law of God—were characterized by "knowledge and understanding." This is an *indirect* reference to illumination, the implication being that they were illumined to have "knowledge and understanding."

WISDOM LITERATURE

Job 20:3   Zophar believed he was illumined by "a spirit," but he wasn't. By implication, this is an *indirect* reference to illumination.

Job 32:7–9 Elihu defined illumination when he attributed his understanding to the "breath of the Almighty." The "breath of the Almighty" is a reference to the Holy Spirit. This is a *direct* reference to the Holy Spirit.

Job 38:36 The LORD asked a rhetorical question to make the point that he alone gives wisdom and understanding. This is an *indirect* reference to illumination with no reference to revelation.

Psalm 19:7–8 The Word of God is the agent for illumination. "Enlightening the eyes" implies the spiritual dynamic that takes place in concert with the Word of God. This is a *direct* reference to illumination.

Psalm 49:3 The psalmist said that meditating will grant understanding. I infer from this that meditating on God's Word provides illumination. This is an *indirect* reference to illumination, having no reference to the Spirit.

Psalm 51:11 David prayed that the Spirit of God would not be taken from him because of his sin. The Holy Spirit illumined David, providing him with wisdom and discernment to rule as king. This is an *indirect* reference to illumination, with no reference to the Word of God.

Psalm 82:5 The psalmist described needy people who are without illumination. The reference to "darkness" could imply spiritual darkness, or being without illumination. This is an *indirect* reference to illumination.

Psalm 89:15 The psalmist spoke of a walk of faith that was represented by the knowledge of God. This is an *indirect* reference to illumination, not specifying the Spirit's work with revelation, but rather the effects.

Psalm 111:10 The psalmist said that fearing the LORD is the way to wisdom and understanding. This is an *indirect* reference to illumination, by implication, and speaks of fearing the LORD, who is revealed by means of the Spirit and the Word of God.

Psalm 119:6 The psalmist could be referring to spiritual eyesight, which implies illumination. This is an *indirect* reference to illumination, with no mention of the Spirit's work.

Psalm 119:11 The psalmist confessed that he put the Word of God in his heart, which could be understood as means for illumination. This is an *indirect* reference to illumination, whereby the Word of God was going into the heart by Spirit-wrought faith.

Psalm 119:15–18   The psalmist prayed for illumination, praying that his spiritual eyes would be enabled to spiritually recognize truth from God's Law. The psalmist affirmed his delight in God's Law, and his affections spawned the desire to be illumined by God's Word. This is a *direct* reference to illumination.

Psalm 119:34–38   The psalmist prayed for understanding, which could be illumination. The result of understanding is obedience. This is an *indirect* reference to illumination.

Psalm 119:43   The psalmist prayed that the Word of God would be in his speech. The implication could be that the psalmist would continue to be illumined. This could be an *indirect* reference to illumination.

Psalm 119:73   The psalmist requested understanding, which could be spiritual illumination. This is an *indirect* reference to illumination, with no mention of the Spirit.

Psalm 119:97–100   The psalmist speaks of the effects experienced from understanding God's Word. This is an *indirect* reference to illumination, where the psalmist meditates on the Law of God and gains understanding. There is no reference to the Spirit's work in providing understanding.

Psalm 119:103–105   The psalmist made clear that he gained understanding through the Word of God. The psalmist characterized the Word of God as a "lamp" and "light," clearly referring to its role as the means of illumining the mind and guiding a person's life. I believe this is a *direct* reference to illumination, where the Word of God affects a person spiritually as a "lamp" and "light."

Psalm 119:125   The psalmist requested understanding, which could be spiritual illumination. This is an *indirect* reference to illumination, with no mention of the Spirit.

Psalm 119:130   The psalmist made a declaration that as the Word of God is studied there is illumination, and understanding is given even for simple-minded people. This is a *direct* reference to illumination.

Psalm 119:144   The psalmist requested understanding, which could be spiritual illumination. This is an *indirect* reference to illumination, with no mention of the Spirit.

Psalm 119:169   The psalmist requested understanding, which could be spiritual illumination. This is an *indirect* reference to illumination, with no mention of the Spirit.

Psalm 139:6–7   The psalmist reveled in the infinite nature of the knowledge of God and yet affirmed the LORD's nearness, citing the presence of his Spirit. This is an *indirect* reference by implication. Only a person who is spiritually illumined recognizes God's infinite knowledge and nearness.

Psalm 143:10   The psalmist relied on God's Spirit to lead him. This was in the context of being taught God's will. These statements, understood in apposition, make it reasonable to categorize them under the doctrine of illumination. This is an *indirect* reference by implication.

Psalm 147:5   The psalmist affirms the Lord's understanding as that which is infinite. Based upon this foundation, God is well qualified to illumine in terms of his right and power. This is an *indirect* reference to illumination by the implication that God is the source of spiritual illumination.

Proverbs 2:2–3   Solomon, who authored Proverbs, exhorts his readers to seek wisdom and understanding. This is an *indirect* reference to illumination, without a reference to the Spirit.

Proverbs 2:5–6   Solomon affirmed that the LORD is the source of knowledge. This is an *indirect* reference to illumination by implication.

Proverbs 3:13   Solomon affirmed the blessing of finding wisdom and understanding. Wisdom and understanding are byproducts of illumination. This is an *indirect* reference to illumination by implication.

PROPHETS

Isaiah 6:9–10   Isaiah, the author, was called by God as a prophet to preach a message that, for many, would not be understood. This is a reference to the Israelites not being illumined, but rather hardened by God's Word. This is an *indirect* reference to illumination.

Isaiah 11:1–3   Isaiah prophesied of Messiah being illumined by God's Spirit. The "Spirit of wisdom … understanding … [and] knowledge" refers to the dynamic of illumination in the mind of Christ. This is an *indirect* reference to illumination.

Isaiah 29:10–11 Isaiah speaks of a judgment on Israel in which they are not illumined. The Word of God is being kept from them. This is an *indirect* reference to illumination.

Isaiah 29:24 Isaiah gave a prophecy that Jerusalem would one day be illumined to understand and believe instruction, which is the Word of God. This is an *indirect* reference to illumination.

Isaiah 34:16 Isaiah exhorts the nations to read God's Word so they will know what the LORD has commanded and how the Spirit is working. The Word of God is the means by which someone is illumined. This is an *indirect* reference to illumination.

Isaiah 37:7 As an act of judgment the LORD prompted his enemies in their spirit. This was not being illumined with truth by the Spirit of the LORD.

Isaiah 40:28 Isaiah spoke of God's infinite understanding. God's mind is infinite, so this is not referring to the same kind of understanding involved in human illumination.

Isaiah 42:1–4 Isaiah prophesied of Messiah being illumined by God's Spirit. This is an *indirect* reference to illumination.

Isaiah 48:16–18 Isaiah, as a prophet, relied on the LORD's Spirit to speak revelation. The LORD, speaking through Isaiah by the Spirit, affirmed his ministry of teaching and guiding. Isaiah, by implication, was illumined by the Spirit, speaking revelation. This is an *indirect* reference to illumination.

Isaiah 59:21 The LORD, through Isaiah, affirmed his covenant with his people, stating that his Spirit was upon them and that his Word was in their mouths. The Spirit of God enabled the Israelites to have access to God's Word. This is an *indirect* reference to illumination.

Isaiah 61:1 This was a messianic prophecy that the Spirit of God would empower Christ's ministry. This is an *indirect* reference to illumination, specifically of the Spirit's role in empowering the Messiah's ministry.

Isaiah 66:2 The LORD, speaking through Isaiah, declares that he will focus on those who are humble toward his Word. This, by implication, *indirectly* refers to illumination, pointing out how a person's disposition must be humble to be blessed.

Jeremiah 15:16 Jeremiah testifies of how the Word of God became a joy to him. It's possible to infer that the Spirit of God illumined Jeremiah to love his Word.

Jeremiah 31:31–33 Jeremiah prophesies of a day when the LORD will "write" the Word of God on the hearts of his people. This is an *indirect* reference to illumination, speaking of believers obeying the Word of God by means of transformed hearts.

Ezekiel 2:1–2 Ezekiel testified that the Spirit entered, and, by implication, enabled him to hear God speak to him. This is a *direct* reference to illumination.

Ezekiel 11:5 At a certain point, the Spirit of the LORD came upon Ezekiel, enabling him to hear God's Word. This is a *direct* reference to illumination.

Ezekiel 11:19–20 Ezekiel prophesied of God's people being converted by being given a new spirit. Once converted, God's people were enabled to understand and obey his Word. This is an *indirect* reference to illumination.

Ezekiel 11:24–25 The Spirit of God enabled Ezekiel to see God's revelation. This is an *indirect* reference to illumination.

Ezekiel 13:3 This was a rebuke to prophets who were not being illumined by God. These prophets, instead of being illumined, looked to themselves for power. This is an *indirect* reference to illumination.

Ezekiel 36:26–27 Ezekiel prophesied of God's people being converted by being given a new spirit. Once converted, God's people were enabled to understand and obey his Word. This is an *indirect* reference to illumination.

Ezekiel 37:14–15 The LORD, speaking through Ezekiel, said that his Spirit would enable his people to know him. This is an *indirect* reference to illumination.

Ezekiel 43:4–7 Ezekiel testified of how the Spirit brought him to a place to hear from the LORD. This, by implication, *indirectly* refers to illumination; one could infer that the Spirit enabled Ezekiel to hear the Word of God.

Daniel 4:8–9 Nebuchadnezzar affirmed that Daniel was a man indwelt by "the spirit of the holy gods" (which in reality could refer to the Holy

Spirit) because he interpreted his dream, which was a revelation from God. This is a *direct* reference to illumination.

Daniel 4:18   Nebuchadnezzar affirmed that Daniel was a man indwelt by "the spirit of the holy gods" (which in reality could refer to the Holy Spirit) because he interpreted his dream, which was a revelation from God. This is a *direct* reference to illumination.

Daniel 5:11–12   Daniel was affirmed as a man indwelt by "the spirit of the holy gods" (which in reality could refer to the Holy Spirit) because he interpreted dreams, which were revelations from God. This is a *direct* reference to illumination.

Daniel 5:14   King Belshazzar affirmed Daniel as a man indwelt by "the spirit of the gods" (which in reality could refer to the Holy Spirit) because he interpreted dreams, which were revelations from God. This is a *direct* reference to illumination.

Daniel 6:3   Daniel was affirmed because he could interpret dreams. This is a *direct* reference to his gift of illumination.

Daniel 9:21–22   Gabriel was sent to give Daniel understanding. This is not necessarily a reference to illumination, but perhaps the LORD, behind the scenes, illumined Daniel, using Gabriel as a facilitator.

Daniel 10:1   The Word of God was revealed to Daniel and he understood this revelation and its implications. This is a *direct* reference to illumination.

Hosea 4:10–11   Hosea spoke of how sin blocks understanding or discernment. This, by implication, *indirectly* refers to illumination, pointing out sin's adverse effects regarding it.

Hosea 4:14   Hosea spoke of those without understanding who ruin themselves by their sin. This, by implication, *indirectly* refers to illumination, pointing out sin's adverse effects regarding it.

Joel 2:28–30   Joel prophesied how the Spirit of God would one day enable men and women to understand revelation. This is an *indirect* reference to illumination.

Obadiah vv. 7–8   Obadiah condemns those who have rejected the LORD;

they are unable to understand, possessing no discernment. This, by implication, *indirectly* speaks of how sin hinders illumination.

Micah 3:8 Micah spoke of how he was empowered by the Spirit to prophesy. This, by implication, *indirectly* speaks of illumination.

Zechariah 4:5–6 Zechariah declared that the Word of the LORD came to Zerubbabel by God's Spirit. This is an *indirect* reference to illumination, whereby the Word is revealed by the Spirit.

Zechariah 7:12 Zechariah spoke of how people hardened their hearts against the Word that was sent by the Spirit. This, by implication, is an *indirect* reference to illumination. The Word works in concert with the Spirit.

Zechariah 12:10 Zechariah spoke of a "spirit of grace" being poured out on the house of David so that God would be revealed to them. This could be an *indirect* reference to illumination, depending on whether you understand "spirit of grace" to be God's Spirit or not.

New Testament

GOSPELS

Matthew 10:20   Jesus commissioned his apostles with confidence that the Spirit would speak through them. This is an *indirect* reference to illumination, implying that the Spirit who gives revelation also enables understanding.

Matthew 11:15   Jesus made this statement to elicit a response from his hearers. This is an *indirect* reference to illumination.

Matthew 11:25–26   Jesus thanked the Father for revealing truth to those who followed him. The Father is the one who is noted as revealing truth; I assume this revelation to be by means of the Spirit. This is *direct* reference to illumination.

Matthew 12:18   The Father put his Spirit upon Jesus to empower his ministry. This, by implication, is an *indirect* reference to illumination, assuming the Spirit illumined Christ's mind to the revelation he proclaimed.

Matthew 13:13–17   Jesus answered his disciples by telling how Isaiah was called by God to preach a message that would not be understood by many. This is a reference to the Israelites not being illumined but hardened by God's Word. This is an *indirect* reference to illumination.

Matthew 15:16   Jesus admonished his hearers for not having understanding. This *indirectly* refers to illumination, illustrating what the hearers did not have.

Matthew 21:42   Jesus quoted a prophetic reference pointing to his crucifixion. This would only be "marvelous" to the "eyes" of those illumined. This, by implication, is an *indirect* reference to illumination.

Matthew 22:28–29   Jesus rebuked the Pharisees for not knowing the Scriptures or God's power. This, by implication is an *indirect* reference to illumination; the Word of God and the power of God (possibly a reference to the Spirit of God) going hand in hand.

Matthew 22:43–44   Jesus speaks of David's ability, enabled by the Spirit, to discern Messianic truth. This is a *direct* reference to illumination.

Mark 7:18   Jesus rebuked the Pharisees for not having understanding.

The unbelieving Pharisees were not illumined to grasp spiritual truth. This is an *indirect* reference to illumination.

Mark 8:17–18 Jesus admonished his hearers for not having understanding. This *indirectly* refers to illumination, illustrating what the hearers did not have.

Mark 12:36 Jesus speaks of David's ability, enabled by the Spirit, to discern Messianic truth. This is a *direct* reference to illumination.

Mark 13:11 Jesus commissioned his apostles with the confidence that the Spirit would speak through them. This is an *indirect* reference to illumination, implying that the Spirit who gives revelation also enables understanding.

Luke 1:15–17 The angel told Zechariah that John the Baptist would be given the Holy Spirit to empower his ministry. This, by implication, is an *indirect* reference to illumination, assuming that the Spirit illumined John the Baptist and the minds of his hearers to understand the revelation he proclaimed.

Luke 1:67 This, by implication, is an *indirect* reference to illumination, assuming the Spirit illumined Zechariah and the minds of his hearers to understand the revelation he proclaimed.

Luke 2:25–32 Simeon was illumined by the Spirit to know that he would see the Messiah. Simeon declared the Messiah to be the illumination to the Gentiles. This is a *direct* reference to illumination.

Luke 4:18 Jesus announced that the Spirit was upon him to empower his ministry of proclamation and healing. This, by implication, is an *indirect* reference to illumination, assuming the Spirit illumined Christ and his hearers to understand the revelation he proclaimed.

Luke 9:44 Jesus exhorted his hearers to be illumined. This is a *direct* reference to illumination.

Luke 10:21 Jesus thanked the Father for revealing truth to those who followed him. The Father is the one who is noted as revealing truth; I assume this revelation to be by means of the Spirit. This is a *direct* reference to illumination.

Luke 12:11–12 Jesus commissioned his apostles with confidence that the Spirit would speak through them. This is an *indirect* reference to illumination, implying that the Spirit who gives revelation also enables understanding.

Luke 24:24–32   When Jesus preached to two disciples on the road to Emmaus, he rebuked them for not believing. Luke, the author of this account, recorded that later these same two had "their eyes ... opened, and [that] they recognized him." The hearts of these disciples burned within them as Jesus explained the Scriptures concerning himself. This is a *direct* reference to illumination, where God opens the minds of hearers to spiritually understand truth.

Luke 24:44–49   Luke recorded that, as Christ preached to his disciples, he "opened their minds to understand the Scriptures." This is a *direct* reference to illumination.

John 1:8–10   John called Jesus the "light, which enlightens." This is an *indirect* reference to illumination in that Christ and his Word are the significant agents for illumination to take place.

John 2:22   John recorded that after Jesus was raised his disciples spiritually responded to the Scripture. This is an *indirect* reference to illumination.

John 4:23–24   Jesus spoke of the internal dynamic that takes place in the spirit of a person when they worship in concert with truth. This, by implication, is an *indirect* reference to illumination, assuming a believer's spirit is moved by the Holy Spirit to worship.

John 5:39–40   Jesus declared that the "Scriptures ... bear witness" about him. This, by implication, is an *indirect* reference to illumination, assuming a believer, by the Holy Spirit, understands truth.

John 6:63   Jesus taught that the Holy Spirit is the one who grants spiritual life through the agency of his spoken Word. This, by implication, is a *direct* reference to illumination, in that it takes place through the agency of the Spirit and teachings of Christ.

John 14:17   Jesus taught that the "Spirit of truth" (a reference to the Holy Spirit) is not received by the sinful world, because the world does not know him. Jesus affirmed that his true disciples know the "Spirit of truth" because he resides in them. This is an *indirect* reference to illumination.

John 14:26   Jesus said to his disciples that the Holy Spirit would teach them and bring truth back to their minds. This is a *direct* reference to the work of illumination.

John 15:26–16:1 Jesus said to his disciples that the Holy Spirit would teach them and bring truth back to their minds, and that they would be empowered to "bear witness" about Christ. This is a *direct* reference to the work of illumination.

John 16:12–15 Jesus said to his disciples that the Holy Spirit would guide them. By virtue of the Spirit being designated the "Spirit of truth," this is an *indirect* reference to the Spirit's role in illumination.

CHURCH HISTORY

Acts 1:2 Luke, the author of Acts, recorded that Jesus taught by means of the Holy Spirit. This, by implication, *indirectly* refers to illumination in that the Holy Spirit is the means by which Christ's teaching would be received and understood.

Acts 2:4 Luke recorded that the Spirit of God gave the disciples revelation to speak. This, by implication, *indirectly* refers to illumination.

Acts 2:17–19 Peter quoted Joel prophesying that the Spirit of God would one day enable men and women to prophesy and understand revelation. This is an *indirect* reference to illumination.

Acts 2:33 Peter preached that the Holy Spirit had enabled his hearers to spiritually see and hear truth. This is a *direct* reference to illumination.

Acts 4:25 Peter preached that David was enabled to prophesy by means of the Spirit. This, by implication, is an *indirect* reference to illumination.

Acts 4:31 Luke records how the early church, "filled with the Holy Spirit," spoke the Word of God. This is an *indirect* reference to illumination, assuming these believers, by the Spirit, had understanding of the revelation they were speaking.

Acts 5:3 By asking why Ananias lied to the Holy Spirit, Peter might have been implying that Ananias had the opportunity to be illumined by the Spirit. This is an *indirect* reference to illumination.

Acts 5:9 By asking why Sapphira tested Spirit, Peter might have been implying that Sapphira had the opportunity to be illumined by the Spirit. This could be an *indirect* reference to illumination.

Acts 5:32 Peter declared that the Holy Spirit is given to believers who obey God. This, by implication, is an *indirect* reference to illumination, in that obedience is spawned by understanding revelation.

Acts 7:51   Stephen condemned the crowd for not being illumined. This is a *direct* reference to illumination.

Acts 7:57   Luke recorded that the crowds plugged their ears, which could be a physical expression that they were not illumined. This, by implication, is an *indirect* reference to illumination.

Acts 8:29–31   Philip inquired of the Ethiopian as to whether or not he understood, which could be taken as a reference to illumination. This, by implication, is an *indirect* reference to illumination.

Acts 9:3–5   Luke records Saul's conversion, in which he was spiritually illumined by Christ. This is a *direct* reference to illumination.

Acts 10:44–47   Luke records that Gentile believers believed by the Spirit and manifested revelation by speaking in tongues. This, by implication, is an *indirect* reference to illumination.

Acts 11:12–17   Luke records that Gentile believers believed by means of the Spirit, being baptized by the Spirit. This, by implication, is an *indirect* reference to illumination.

Acts 11:28   Agabus was given revelation by the Spirit. This, by implication, is an *indirect* reference to illumination.

Acts 13:2–4   The Holy Spirit spoke to the early church, giving direct revelation. This, by implication, is an *indirect* reference to illumination.

Acts 15:28   The apostles at the Jerusalem council affirmed the direction the Holy Spirit gave to them. This, by implication, is an *indirect* reference to illumination.

Acts 16:6–7   The Spirit directed Paul and Silas on their missionary journey. This, by implication, is an *indirect* reference to illumination.

Acts 17:20   Paul preached in Athens to some who were not illumined and who were calling the truth strange. This, by implication, is an *indirect* reference to illumination.

Acts 18:25   Paul preached with fervency "in spirit," believing his message in earnest. This, by implication, is an *indirect* reference to illumination.

Acts 19:6   Luke records that Paul had preached to disciples of John who believed by means of the Spirit and were being baptized by the Spirit. This, by implication, is an *indirect* reference to illumination manifesting revelatory gifts.

Acts 19:21   The Spirit directed Paul to back to Jerusalem, and then ultimately to Rome. This, by implication, is an *indirect* reference to illumination.

Acts 21:4   The disciples, illumined by the Spirit, warned Paul not to go to Jerusalem. This is a *direct* reference to illumination.

Acts 21:11   Agabus, by the Spirit, spoke revelation concerning Paul's destination. This, by implication, is an *indirect* reference to illumination.

Acts 22:6–11   As a prisoner Paul testified concerning his conversion to the mob in Jerusalem. Paul described his conversion as being spiritually illumined by the Lord. This is a *direct* reference to illumination.

Acts 22:17–18   Paul fell into a trance and saw the Lord Jesus directly giving him revelation. This, by implication, is an *indirect* reference to illumination.

Acts 26:12–18   Paul testified to King Agrippa of his conversion whereby he was spiritually illumined by the Lord. The Lord Jesus commissioned Paul to be a witness to the Gentiles so that they too would be illumined. This is a *direct* reference to illumination.

Acts 28:25–27   Paul preached in Rome and quoted Isaiah 6:9 as a condemnation of people unable to spiritually discern truth. This is an *indirect* reference to illumination, in that some were not illumined to spiritually see or hear truth.

EPISTLES

Romans 1:16–17   Paul declared that the gospel is the power for salvation for those who believe. Within the gospel, righteousness is revealed. This is a *direct* reference to illumination wherein the gospel reveals God's righteousness.

Romans 8:4–11   Paul taught the believer to be spiritually minded. This, by implication, is an *indirect* reference to illumination.

Romans 8:13–16   Paul taught that believers receive, by the Spirit, the assurance that they are adopted as children of God. By the illumination of the Holy Spirit, a believer's spirit or inner man resonates with the Holy Spirit, bringing assurance of salvation and confidence in his or her relationship to God. This is a *direct* reference to the doctrine of illumination.

Romans 8:26–27   Paul describes the spiritual dynamic between the believer's weakness and the intercessory ministry of the Holy Spirit. The Spirit of God aligns the believer's prayers with the will of God. This, by implication, is an *indirect* reference to illumination.

Romans 9:1   Paul testified that he was telling the truth by the illuminating Holy Spirit. This is a *direct* reference to the doctrine of illumination.

Romans 10:14–18   Paul taught that faith comes from hearing the Word of Christ. This, by implication, is an *indirect* reference to illumination.

Romans 11:8   Paul taught that the Jews, being under God's judgment, were rendered unable to see or hear truth. This is the opposite of being illumined by the Spirit to perceive truth. This, by implication, is an *indirect* reference to illumination.

Romans 15:13   Paul gave a doxology to the church, speaking of the Holy Spirit's power to fill believers with hope. This is an *indirect* reference to illumination.

Romans 16:25–26   Paul taught that the gospel is a revelation of something that was hidden before but is now known to the nations. This, by implication, is an *indirect* reference to illumination.

1 Corinthians 2:4   Paul reported that his preaching was a demonstration of the Spirit. To comprehend Paul's preaching, one must be illumined by the Spirit. This, by implication, is an *indirect* reference to illumination.

1 Corinthians 2:9–16   Paul taught that the way to comprehend spiritual truth is by the Spirit of God. Paul taught that the Spirit of God is the only Being credentialed by his knowledge of God to illumine the mind of man. This is a *direct* reference to the doctrine of illumination.

1 Corinthians 12:3   Paul taught that a person speaking by the Holy Spirit cannot curse Jesus, and a person cannot praise Jesus except by the Holy Spirit. Paul taught that praising or cursing the Lord had to do with whether a person was illumined by the Spirit or not. This, by implication, is an *indirect* reference to the doctrine of illumination.

1 Corinthians 12:4–8   Paul taught that spiritual gifts are given through the Spirit, and that particular gifts are revelatory. These gifts are related to the doctrine of illumination, in that one gifted in this way knows revelation by means of the Spirit.

1 Corinthians 12:10–11 Paul taught that spiritual gifts were given through the Spirit and that particular gifts were revelatory. These gifts are related to the doctrine of illumination, in that one gifted in this way knows revelation by means of the Spirit.

1 Corinthians 13:2 Paul taught that it was essential to possess love, no matter a person's spiritual giftedness. This, by implication, is an *indirect* reference to the doctrine of illumination.

1 Corinthians 13:9–12 Paul taught that full knowledge is for those who are glorified. This, by implication, is an *indirect* reference to the doctrine of illumination.

1 Corinthians 14:6 Paul taught that it was unfruitful to use one's prophetic gift if it was unintelligible or devoid of knowledge. Paul taught that revelation must have content. This, by implication, is an *indirect* reference to the doctrine of illumination.

1 Corinthians 14:12–16 Paul taught that it was unfruitful to use one's prophetic gift if it was unintelligible or devoid of knowledge. Paul taught that revelation must have content. This, by implication, is an *indirect* reference to the doctrine of illumination.

1 Corinthians 14:26–30 Paul taught that it was unfruitful to use one's prophetic gift if it was unintelligible or devoid of knowledge. Paul taught that revelation must have content. This, by implication, is an *indirect* reference to the doctrine of illumination.

2 Corinthians 3:3–9 Paul taught that the church possesses a ministry of the Spirit. Paul implied by this that new-covenant believers have been illumined by the Holy Spirit. This, by implication, is an *indirect* reference to the doctrine of illumination.

2 Corinthians 3:17–18 Paul taught that believers were illumined by the Spirit of God to behold "the glory of the Lord." Such believers were being transformed in holiness. This is a *direct* reference to the doctrine of illumination.

2 Corinthians 4:2–6 Paul taught that the gospel is veiled to those who do not believe. Paul also taught that by hearing Christ proclaimed a person can be illumined to belief—to seeing the glory of Christ by faith. This is a *direct* reference to the doctrine of illumination.

2 Corinthians 4:13   Paul taught that belief is initiated by preaching. Belief is predicated on illumination. This, by implication, is an *indirect* reference to the doctrine of illumination.

Galatians 1:11–12   Paul taught that he received the gospel through a revelation of Jesus Christ. Paul was illumined by God to believe. This is an *indirect* reference to the doctrine of illumination.

Galatians 2:2   Paul testified that he had been given a revelation of the gospel by God. This is an *indirect* reference to the doctrine of illumination.

Galatians 3:2–5   Paul taught that God supplied the Spirit to the church. This is an *indirect* reference to the doctrine of illumination.

Galatians 3:14   Paul taught that all who receive the Spirit do so through faith. This is an *indirect* reference to the doctrine of illumination.

Galatians 4:6   Paul affirmed that believers are given confidence in their sonship by means of the Holy Spirit. This is a *direct* reference to the doctrine of illumination.

Galatians 5:5   Paul taught that, by the Spirit and by believing, believers anticipate heaven. This is an *indirect* reference to the doctrine of illumination.

Ephesians 1:13–14   Paul taught that believers are given the Holy Spirit as a guarantee of their salvation. By the Spirit's illumination, believers know they are promised salvation. This is an *indirect* reference to the doctrine of illumination.

Ephesians 1:17–18   Paul taught that, because believers are regenerate, they can be illumined to greater spiritual realities. This is a *direct* reference to the doctrine of illumination.

Ephesians 2:18   Paul taught that believers have access to the Father by means of the Spirit. This is an *indirect* reference to the doctrine of illumination.

Ephesians 3:3   Paul testified that the mystery of the gospel was made known to him by revelation. This is a *direct* reference to the doctrine of illumination.

Ephesians 3:4–5   Paul testified that the mystery of the gospel was made known to him by revelation. This is a *direct* reference to the doctrine of illumination.

Ephesians 3:16–21   Paul prayed for the Ephesians to be illumined by the power of God to know the love of Christ. This is a *direct* reference to the doctrine of illumination.

Ephesians 4:18   Paul referred to unbelievers as those without illumined minds. This is an *indirect* reference to the doctrine of illumination.

Ephesians 4:22–23   Paul taught that believers are to have renewed minds through the knowledge of Christ. This is an *indirect* reference to the doctrine of illumination.

Ephesians 5:9–10   Paul taught that believers must possess discernment that is based on righteous living. This is an *indirect* reference to the doctrine of illumination.

Ephesians 5:17–18   Paul taught that believers are to pursue God's will, avoid returning to party-living, and allow themselves to be illumined by the Holy Spirit. This is a *direct* reference to the doctrine of illumination.

Ephesians 6:17–19   When Paul described the spiritual weapon of "the sword of the Spirit," he was teaching that the Spirit of God is inextricably linked to the Word of God. This, by implication, is an *indirect* reference to the doctrine of illumination.

Philippians 1:8–9   Paul desired that the believers in this church would grow in their spiritual knowledge and spiritual discernment. This is an *indirect* reference to the doctrine of illumination.

Philippians 3:3   Paul defined believers as those who worship by means of the Spirit of God. Only believers illumined by the Spirit worship by the Spirit. This is an *indirect* reference to the doctrine of illumination.

Colossians 1:4–6   Paul taught that believers, by grace, first have to come to an understanding of the truth. This is an *indirect* reference to the doctrine of illumination.

Colossians 1:9–10   Paul prayed that these believers would be illumined by the truth and would grow both in knowledge and in pleasing the Lord. This is a *direct* reference to the doctrine of illumination.

Colossians 1:12–13   Paul described Christianity as a deliverance from darkness to light. This is an *indirect* reference to the doctrine of illumination.

Colossians 2:2–3   Paul's desire was for these believers, by illumination, to gain clear knowledge and assurance from the gospel. This is a *direct* reference to the doctrine of illumination.

Colossians 3:10   Paul taught that spiritual renewal comes by means of knowledge. This is an *indirect* reference to the doctrine of illumination.

Colossians 3:16   Paul desired for the teachings of Christ to be deeply rooted in the hearts of these believers so as to produce spiritual wisdom and spiritual responses. This is a *direct* reference to the doctrine of illumination.

1 Thessalonians 1:4–6   Paul affirmed these believers' salvation based upon the way the gospel was empowered by the Spirit. This is an *indirect* reference to the doctrine of illumination.

1 Thessalonians 2:13   Paul affirmed these believers as those who received God's Word, preached by Paul and others, as actually being God's Word. Paul also affirmed that the Word of God works in believers. This, by implication, is an *indirect* reference to the doctrine of illumination.

1 Thessalonians 4:6–8   Paul taught that to disregard obedience is to disregard conviction by the Holy Spirit. This, by implication, is an *indirect* reference to the doctrine of illumination, because the Spirit of God illumines a person regarding his or her sin.

1 Thessalonians 5:18–20   Paul taught that believers can quench or remove the effect of the Spirit within a worship setting. This, by implication, is an *indirect* reference to the doctrine of illumination, because the Spirit is the one who enlightens the Scripture in a person's mind, and this verse speaks of the effectiveness of illumination.

2 Thessalonians 2:13   Paul taught that sanctification by means of the Spirit and believing in the truth go hand in hand. This is an *indirect* reference to illumination.

1 Timothy 2:4   Paul taught that when a person is saved he or she is illumined—able to know the truth. This is a *direct* reference to illumination.

2 Timothy 1:14   Paul taught that the Holy Spirit is the agent by which leaders in the church are enabled to discern how to guard the gospel. This is an *indirect* reference to illumination.

2 Timothy 2:7   Paul exhorted Timothy to think about what he had just taught, on the assumption that the Lord would illumine his mind to understand the truth. This is a *direct* reference to illumination.

2 Timothy 2:25   Paul taught that correcting opponents could facilitate repentance and then illumination to know the truth. This is a *direct* reference to illumination.

2 Timothy 3:7   Paul taught that false teachers learn but are never illumined. This is an *indirect* reference to illumination.

2 Timothy 3:15–16   Paul reminded Timothy of the Scripture's power and how it enabled Timothy to gain the wisdom for salvation. This is an *indirect* reference to illumination.

Titus 1:1   Paul acknowledged the believers under Titus's ministry as those who possessed "knowledge of the truth." This was more than intellectual knowledge; it was illumined knowledge of inspired Scripture. This is an *indirect* reference to illumination.

Hebrews 3:7–8   The author of Hebrews quoted Psalm 95:7–11 to warn his hearers not to harden their hearts. The author stated that the Holy Spirit was saying this to this church, and that this was an example of how God's Word was shared for the purpose of spiritual illumination. This, by implication, is an *indirect* reference to illumination.

Hebrews 4:12   The author of Hebrews described the dynamic convicting ministry of the Word of God in the believer's heart. This, by implication, is an *indirect* reference to illumination, showing that believers are enlightened regarding their sin.

Hebrews 6:4–6   The author of Hebrews warned the church that a person exposed to the power of God can experience levels of spiritual enlightenment by the Holy Spirit, which, if rejected, will harden the heart.

Appendix

This enlightenment is not the illumination a believer receives, because the receptor is still in darkness; instead of believing truth, the person rejects truth. This is an *indirect* reference to illumination.

Hebrews 9:8 The author of Hebrews explained that the Holy Spirit had made known information regarding old covenant tabernacle worship. This, by implication, is an *indirect* reference to illumination.

Hebrews 10:15–17 The author of Hebrews indicated that the Holy Spirit had illumined Jeremiah 31:33 to him so that he could apply it in a new-covenant context. This is a *direct* reference to illumination.

Hebrews 10:26 The author of Hebrews warned the church that a person who receives spiritual knowledge of the truth and rejects it will be rejected by God. Such a person has not received this knowledge by faith and is not truly illumined. This is an *indirect* reference to illumination.

James 1:18 James made it clear that the vehicle for spiritual birth is by means of the Scripture. This is an *indirect* reference to illumination.

James 1:23–25 James made it clear that a person who genuinely hears the Word of God responds to the Word of God. This, by implication, is an *indirect* reference to illumination.

James 3:13 James asked this rhetorical question regarding the spiritual status of those in the church. He indicated that a person who is characteristically wise or possesses understanding will show it by a lifestyle of humility and discernment. This, by implication, is an *indirect* reference to illumination.

James 4:5 James asked this rhetorical question so the church would recognize that a person who loves the world loses his or her spiritual intimacy with God. This, by implication, is an *indirect* reference to illumination.

1 Peter 1:10–12 Peter wrote to the church that the prophets, by the Spirit, had some indication of the salvation that their Messiah would bring. This is a *direct* reference to the doctrine of illumination.

1 Peter 1:13 Peter exhorted the church to prepare their minds for Christ to be revealed at his return. Peter identified the unique way Christ will be revealed to believers when he returns. This is an *indirect* reference to the doctrine of illumination.

1 Peter 1:23 Peter made it clear that the vehicle for spiritual birth is Scripture. This is an *indirect* reference to the doctrine of illumination.

1 Peter 2:2–3 Peter taught that believers taste the Word of God. This could be a reference to the spiritual dynamic that takes place when a person is illumined by the Scripture. This is an *indirect* reference to the doctrine of illumination.

2 Peter 1:3 Peter wrote that God's sanctifying power comes through the knowledge of God. This is an *indirect* reference to the doctrine of illumination.

2 Peter 1:15–21 Peter affirmed that Scripture, rather than spiritual experience, is the means of illumination. This is a *direct* reference to the doctrine of illumination.

2 Peter 2:20 Peter affirmed that God's power for sanctification comes through the knowledge of God. This is an *indirect* reference to illumination.

2 Peter 3:15–16 Peter affirmed that Paul's writings were given to him through wisdom, which refers to the inspiration of the Holy Spirit (see 2 Tim. 3:16). This is an *indirect* reference to illumination.

2 Peter 3:18 Peter wrote that God's power for sanctification comes through growing in knowledge of God. This is an *indirect* reference to illumination.

1 John 2:8 John referred to the light that has come with the coming of Christ. Believers are illumined by the light of the gospel. This is an *indirect* reference to illumination.

1 John 2:20 John affirmed that believers can understand truth because of their anointing from the Holy Spirit. This is a *direct* reference to illumination.

1 John 2:27 John affirmed that believers can understand truth because of their anointing from the Holy Spirit. This is a *direct* reference to illumination.

1 John 3:24 John taught that the Spirit of God brings assurance to true believers. This is an *indirect* reference to illumination.

1 John 4:1–6 John taught that true believers have spiritual discernment and are able to tell the difference between the truth and error. The genuine believer "listens" to truth. This is an *indirect* reference to illumination.

1 John 4:13   John taught that the Spirit of God brings assurance to true believers. This is an *indirect* reference to illumination.

1 John 5:6–11   John taught that the Spirit and the truth are inextricably linked. John taught that the Spirit of God brings assurance to true believers. The "testimony" is a *direct* reference to illumination.

1 John 5:20   John taught that the Spirit of God brings assurance to true believers. The "understanding" that a believer has is an *indirect* reference to illumination.

Jude v. 20   Jude exhorted believers to pray by means of the Holy Spirit. This, by implication, is an *indirect* reference to illumination.

Revelation 1:1   John testified that Jesus was revealed to him in a vision. This revelation is, by implication, an *indirect* reference to illumination.

Revelation 1:3   John affirmed believers who are able to hear this prophecy, which is truth. Hearing could be a reference to illumination. This is an *indirect* reference to illumination.

Revelation 1:10   John affirmed that he was able to hear this prophecy, which is truth. Hearing was illumination. This is a *direct* reference to illumination.

Revelation 2:7, 11, 17, 29; 3:1, 6, 13   John exhorted believers to be open to hearing from the Spirit of God, who was directly connected to the prophecy John was writing. This is an *indirect* reference to the doctrine of illumination.

Revelation 4:1–2   John testified to being caught up in a vision by the Holy Spirit. This, by implication, is an *indirect* reference to the doctrine of illumination.

Revelation 19:10   John referred to the spiritual nature of the truth. This, by implication, has *indirect* bearing on the doctrine of illumination.

Revelation 21:10   John testified that he was shown this prophecy by means of the Spirit. This, by implication, is an *indirect* reference to the doctrine of illumination.

Revelation 22:17   The Spirit of God calls believers to believe. Genuine believers will spiritually thirst for the truth. This is an *indirect* reference to the doctrine of illumination.

Revelation 22:18–19 John warned those who might hear and reject truth by adding to it or taking away from it. Hearing and not believing brings condemnation. This is an *indirect* reference to the doctrine of illumination, as it describes the opposite.

Conclusion

As the research reflects, the doctrine of illumination spans the Scriptures. My conclusion is that God has clearly spoken regarding the way in which he opens the minds of people to his Word. I see four categories into which these scriptural references fall regarding the role of illumination:

* *condemnation*, referring to the person who is without illumination and is rejecting the Word of God
* *conversion*, speaking of the transformation that takes place when God changes a heart and gives illumination
* *communication*, speaking of how prophets, preachers, and evangelists are illumined to preach God's Word, and how hearers are illumined by the preaching of God's Word
* *convictions*, which are gained as believers are enriched in their own spiritual walks, acquiring greater certainty and affection over spiritual truth as they are illumined by the Spirit and his Word.

Appendix

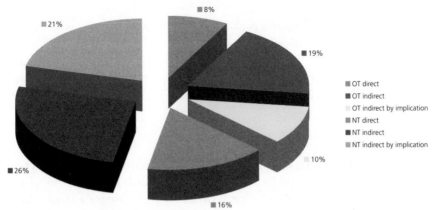

OT direct
OT indirect
OT indirect by implication
NT direct
NT indirect
NT indirect by implication

Breakdown of OT/NT illumination references

Breakdown of illumination references by OT/NT

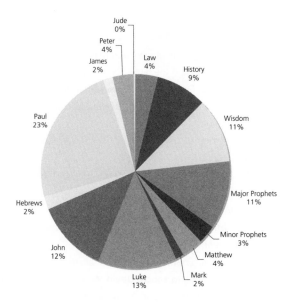

Breakdown of illumination references by genre/author

Bibliography

Anderson, Kent, review of Craddock, *As One Without Authority*, at: preaching.org

——Review of Doug Pagitt, *Preaching Re-Imagined*, at: preaching.org

Averbeck, Richard E., "God, People, and the Bible: The Relationship between Illumination and Biblical Scholarship," in **Wallace, Daniel B.,** and **Sawyer M. James,** (eds.), *Who's Afraid of the Holy Spirit? An Investigation into the Ministry of the Spirit of God Today* (Dallas: Biblical Studies Press, 2005)

Berkhof, Hendrikus, *The Doctrine of the Holy Spirit: The Annie Kinkead Warfield Lectures, 1963–1964* (Richmond, VA: John Knox Press, 1964)

BibleWorks 6: Software for Biblical Exegesis and Research, CD-ROM (Norfolk, VA: BibleWorks, LLC, 2005)

Calvin, John, *Calvin: Institutes of the Christian Religion*, vols. xx and xxi of **Baillie, John, McNeill, John T.,** and **Van Dusen, Henry P.,** (eds.), *The Library of Christian Classics* (Louisville, KY: Westminster John Knox Press, 1960)

——and **Parker, T. H. L.,** (tr.), *The Epistles of Paul the Apostle to the Galatians, Ephesians, Philippians and Colossians*, vol. ii of **Torrance, David W.,** and **Torrance, Thomas F.,** (eds.), *Calvin's New Testament Commentaries* (Grand Rapids, MI: Eerdmans, 1965)

——"Geneva Catechism," in **Torrance, Thomas F.,** (ed. and tr.), *The School of Faith: The Catechisms of the Reformed Church* (Eugene, OR: Wipf and Stock, 1959)

——and **Beveridge, Henry,** (tr.), *Tracts and Treatises on the Doctrine and Worship of the Church* (1849; 1958, Grand Rapids, MI: Eerdmans)

Craddock, Fred B., *As One Without Authority* (St. Louis, MI: Chalice Press, 2001)

——"Preaching: An Appeal to Memory," in **Graves, Mike,** (ed.), *What's the Matter with Preaching Today?* (Louisville, KY: Westminster John Knox Press, 2004)

Dillenberger, John, (ed.), Introduction, *John Calvin: Selections from his Writings* ([n.p.]: Scholars Press for the American Academy of Religion, 1975)

Edwards, Jonathan, *The Religious Affections* (1746; 1986, Carlisle, PA: Banner of Truth)

Farris, Stephen, review of **Craddock,** *As One Without Authority*, in *Homiletic*, 27/1 (2002), pp. 35–36

Hargrove, Carl A., "The Role of the Holy Spirit as Convictor and Supporter in Preaching," Master's thesis, The Master's Seminary, 2006

Heisler, Greg, *Spirit-Led Preaching: The Holy Spirit's Role in Sermon Preparation and Delivery* (Nashville: B & H Academic, 2007)

Hodge, Charles, *Commentary on the Second Epistle to the Corinthians* (1864; n.d., Grand Rapids, MI: Eerdmans)

——*Ephesians* (The Geneva Series of Commentaries; 1856; 1991, Carlisle, PA: Banner of Truth)

Hoehner, Harold, *Ephesians: An Exegetical Commentary* (Grand Rapids, MI: Baker Academic, 2002)

Kaiser, Walter, "The Power of the Word of God," sermon preached at The Bible Church of Little Rock, October 22, 2006, at: http://64.19.50.210/Default.aspx

Kent, Homer A., Jr., *Ephesians: The Glory of the Church* (Everyman's Bible Commentary; Chicago: Moody Press, 1971)

Kierkegaard, Søren, and **Hong, Howard V.,** and **Hong, Edna H.,** (tr. and eds.), *For Self-Examination* in *Kierkegaard's Writings,* vol. xxi (1851; 1990, Princeton: Princeton University Press)

Larsen, David L., *The Company of Preachers: A History of Biblical Preaching from the Old Testament to the Modern Era* (Grand Rapids, MI: Kregel, 1998)

Lloyd-Jones, D. Martyn, *Preaching and Preachers* (1971; 1985, London: Hodder and Stoughton)

Mohler, Albert, "Why Do We Preach? A Foundation for Christian Preaching, Part One," December 15, 2005, "Commentary," at: AlbertMohler.com

Mueller, J. Theodore, "The Holy Spirit and the Scriptures," in Henry, Carl F. H., (ed.), *Revelation and the Bible: Contemporary Evangelical Thought* (Grand Rapids, MI: Baker, 1958)

Nichols, Stephen J., *An Absolute Sort of Certainty: The Holy Spirit and the Apologetics of Jonathan Edwards* (Phillipsburg, NJ: P & R, 2003)

Owen, John, *The Holy Spirit: His Gifts and Power* (Grand Rapids, MI: Kregel, 1954)

——and **Goold, William H.,** (ed.), *The Works of John Owen,* vol. iv (1850; 1967, London: Banner of Truth)

Ownes, R. Eugene, review of **Fred Craddock,** *As One Without Authority,* in *Perspectives in Religious Studies,* 7/3 (1980), pp. 246–247

Pache, René, and **Needham, Helen I.,** (tr.),*The Inspiration and Authority of Scripture* (1969; 1992, Salem, WI: Sheffield Publishing)

Packer, J. I., "Calvin the Theologian," in **Duffield, G. E.,** (ed.), *John Calvin: A Collection of Essays* (London: Sutton Courtenay Press, 1966)

——*God Has Spoken* (Grand Rapids, MI: Baker, 1988)

Pagitt, Doug, *Preaching Re-Imagined: The Role of the Sermon in Communities of Faith* (Grand Rapids, MI: Zondervan, 2005)

Pascal, Blaise, and **Trotter, W. F.,** (tr.), *Pensées,* (New York: Random House, 1941)

Piper, John, "The Divine Majesty of the Word: John Calvin, The Man and His Preaching," Bethlehem Conference for Pastors, February 4, 1997

——*Seeing and Savoring Jesus Christ* (Wheaton, IL: Crossway, 2004)

Bibliography

Ramm, Bernard L., *Rapping about the Spirit* (Waco, TX: Word, 1974)

Reid, Robert Stephen, *"Preaching Re-Imagined: The Role of the Sermon in Communities of Faith,"* in *The Christian Century*, August 22, 2006

Ridderbos, Herman, and **de Witt, John Richard,** (tr.), *Paul: An Outline of his Theology* (1966; 1975, Grand Rapids, MI: Eerdmans)

Rowell, Andy, "Review of *Preaching Re-Imagined* by Doug Pagitt," Church Leadership Conversations, February 26, 2006, at: andyrowell.net

Shivers, Mark, "Preaching Re-Imagined: A Review," at: theOoze.com

Sproul, R. C., "The Internal Testimony of the Holy Spirit," in Geisler, Norman L., (ed.), *Inerrancy* (Grand Rapids, MI: Zondervan, 1980)

Vanhoozer, Kevin J., *Is There a Meaning in This Text? The Bible, the Reader, and the Morality of Literary Knowledge* (Grand Rapids, MI: Zondervan, 1998)

Warfield, B. B., *Calvin and Augustine* (1956; 1980, Philadelphia: P & R, 1980)

Zemek, George J., *The Word of God in the Child of God: Exegetical, Theological, and Homiletical Reflections from the 119th Psalm* (Mango, FL: n.p.; n.d.)

About Day One:

Day One's threefold commitment:

- TO BE FAITHFUL TO THE BIBLE, GOD'S INERRANT, INFALLIBLE WORD;

- TO BE RELEVANT TO OUR MODERN GENERATION;

- TO BE EXCELLENT IN OUR PUBLICATION STANDARDS.

I continue to be thankful for the publications of Day One. They are biblical; they have sound theology; and they are relative to the issues at hand. The material is condensed and manageable while, at the same time, being complete—a challenging balance to find. We are happy in our ministry to make use of these excellent publications.

JOHN MACARTHUR, PASTOR-TEACHER, GRACE COMMUNITY CHURCH, CALIFORNIA

It is a great encouragement to see Day One making such excellent progress. Their publications are always biblical, accessible and attractively produced, with no compromise on quality. Long may their progress continue and increase!

JOHN BLANCHARD, AUTHOR, EVANGELIST AND APOLOGIST

Visit our website for more information and to request a free catalogue of our books.

www.dayone.co.uk

A practical theology of missions
Dispelling the mystery,
recovering the passion

ERIC E. WRIGHT

384PP PAPERBACK

978–1–84625–198–6

↑MINISTRY
MISSION→

A Practical
Theology of Missions

Dispelling the mystery;
Recovering the passion

Eric E Wright   DayOne

What is the church's work of missions, and how should we carry it out? In this thorough study, Eric Wright roots missions solidly in the biblical text while giving modern, real-life examples of how missionary principles can be applied practically. He covers subjects such as missions and God's kingdom, the validity of mission boards, the role of providence, the necessary spiritual gifts, the multi-ethnic nature of ideal churches, how to avoid dependency, the priority of church planting versus humanitarian ministries, and short-term versus life-long missionary commitment.

A good understanding of biblical theology provides the basis for effective cross-cultural missionary work in *A Practical Theology of Missions* ... I highly recommend his effort.
RUDOLPH H. WIEBE, LECTURER AT THE TORONTO BAPTIST SEMINARY FOR TWENTY-NINE YEARS AND A PRINCIPAL LECTURER AT THE FEDERAL COLLEGE OF EDUCATION, PANKSHIN, NIGERIA, WEST AFRICA SINCE 2004.

This book is the climax of Eric Wright's full life as missionary, pastor and author ... It

distils decades of missionary experience and research, reflection and devotion. The book is thorough and balanced, and yet it is an inspiring book to read.
REVD GEOFF THOMAS, PASTOR SINCE 1965 OF ALFRED PLACE BAPTIST CHURCH, ABERYSTWYTH, WALES, UK

Eric E. Wright grew up in Toronto, Canada. He and his wife, Mary Helen, were called to missionary service in the Muslim world, ministering in Pakistan for sixteen years. There Eric became co-founder of the Open Theological Seminary. After returning to Canada, Eric pastored Long Branch Baptist Church, Toronto, served as interim pastor in six other churches, and taught both the history and theology of missions at Toronto Baptist Seminary. Eric and Mary Helen have three married children and nine grandchildren. They live in Salem, Ontario.

Exemplary spiritual leadership
Facing the challenges, escaping the dangers

JERRY WRAGG

MINISTRY AND MISSION SERIES

144PP PAPERBACK

978–1–84625–200–6

What is it that compels a group of people to follow the leadership and vision of one person? Why are the insights and pursuits of certain individuals more persuasive than those of others?

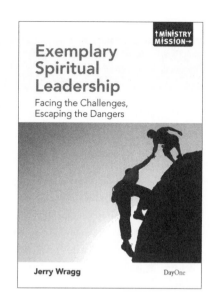

In this book, Jerry Wragg investigates how leadership should be characterized in the church, and how biblical leadership must differ from the kind of leadership promoted in the world. He explores the dynamics of leadership, particularly the character traits that need to be built up or eradicated in leaders, the dangers that leaders face and temptations to which they are particularly prone, and the development of future leaders: how to recognize leadership potential and encourage leadership gifts in the next generation. Throughout, Jerry Wragg writes honestly and offers pastoral encouragement and practical guidance that will help all men placed in church leadership positions.

Jerry Wragg was born and raised in California. Although exposed to Christian training through his parents' example and his own involvement in church, he didn't come to faith in Christ until after he was married and serving in the United States Air Force. After he was discharged, he graduated from The Master's Seminary with a Masters degree in Ministry and served as an associate pastor and personal assistant to Dr. John MacArthur at Grace Community Church, California. In 2001, he accepted the call to be pastor-teacher at Grace Immanuel Bible Church in Jupiter, Florida, where he is currently ministering. He has taught on church leadership, biblical counseling, theology and Bible survey courses, marriage and family, and parenting. In addition, Jerry serves as Board Chairman for The Expositors Seminary, Jupiter, Florida. He and his wife, Louise, have four adult children and are the proud grandparents of three grandsons and one granddaughter.

Forthcoming

Biblical shepherding of God's sheep
The use and abuse of authority
by church officers

MARTIN, STEVEN (ED.)

978-1-84625-195-5

Biblical Shepherding of God's sheep

The use and abuse of authority by church officers

Steve Martin, Editor   DayOne

"Tend my sheep" is the awesome task given to those who have been called and equipped by the Holy Spirit to be overseers of the church of God. Leadership in the local assembly must be biblical and balanced if the church is to properly discharge its commission from the Lord Jesus Christ.

Recent trends in leadership methods have made it more necessary than ever that Christ's shepherds "be on guard for yourselves and for all the flock." The application of biblical church authority is one of the crucial issues facing Christians today.

This work deals forthrightly with the hard questions about leading God's people on the local-church level. Representing the mature thought of men who have spent many years guiding Christians, Biblical Shepherding of God's Sheep is an anthology of essays dealing with various aspects of the issue of church authority. The true nature of an "ideal" church, the proper way of reformation, the danger of the abuse of church discipline and the relationship of authority to individual freedom are some of the topics handled here.

Leaders reproduce themselves and put their stamp indelibly upon a congregation. This influence can in turn make or break a church's influence in the world. These essays provide the tools needed for the self-examination, correction and growth of all those concerned to see Christ's style of shepherding safeguarded among his flock.

Contains contributions from:

Leon Blosser,

Walter Chantry

Paul Clarke

Erroll Hulse

Donald R. Lindblad

Steven L. Martin

Thomas Nettles

Henry Rast

Ernest Reisinger

James Renihan

John Thornbury